The Other Side Of Desire

Author:
Samuel O. Mbisike

Copyright © SAMUEL O. MBISIKE 2011
All rights reserved.
No part of this publication may be produced, distributed, or transmitted in any form or by any means, including photocopying, recording, or other electronic or mechanical methods, without the prior written permission of the publisher, except in the case of brief quotations embodied in critical reviews and certain other noncommercial uses permitted by copyright law.

For permission requests, write to the publisher, addressed "Attention: Permissions Coordinator" at the email address below:

Life and Success Media Ltd
e-mail: info@abookinsideyou.com
www.lifeandsuccesspublishing.com

ISBN: 978-1-64764-477-2
Cover Design: Allan Sealy

Dedication

Sheila And Lawrence Madu

Content

Foreword 9

Acknowledgement 11

Introduction 13

Chapter 1:
Microwave Love 17

Chapter 2:
Shattered Dreams 25

Chapter 3:
Even With Flowers 31

Chapter 4:
Loneliness   43

Chapter 5:
Loving The Wrong Person   51

Chapter 6:
Single By Choice   59

Chapter 7:
Hiv/aids And Health Implications   67

Chapter 8:
Single Parenthood   73

Chapter 9:
Puzzling   87

Chapter 10:
Tears For Love   93

Chapter 11:
Crazy Love   99

Chapter12:
Romantic Rejection   105

Chapter 13:
Teen Pregnancy   113

Content

Chapter 14:
Dashed Hopes   119

Chapter 15:
Choosing A Partner   125

Chapter 16:
Partner Choices And Consequences   137

Chapter 17:
Irony Of Wedding Vows   147

Chapter 18:
Multiple Sex Partners   153

Chapter 19:
Divorce   161

Foreword

The book "The Other Side of Desire" written by Samuel O. Mbisike is a great expose on the despicable turbulence which persons of both sexes could go through when caution is not exercised in relationship cravings.

The book is necessary at this time when the world is experiencing unspeakable domestic violence, high divorce rates and spousal homicide with their attendant health implications. Legitimate curiosity on the transient nature of romantic love is the propelling force in the writing of this book.

This is a must read book because it throws light on the intricacies of desire and its other sides; so that cautious optimism would be exercised in establishing relationship ties.

This dynamic stride which covers multi disciplines gives enriching insight into the many factors to be considered before consummating relationships or saying "I do."

Samuel is a Law undergraduate in the United States of America and has demonstrated tremendous mastery of the subject.

Bridget O. Juwah
President Health Foundation
California, USA.

Acknowledgement

I give glory to Almighty God for the successful production of this book.

Immense thanks go to my parents and siblings for monumental support and love through the course of my life and through the production of this book.

I want to appreciate Pastors Antoni and Lucy Okoh, Pastor Yomi and Taye Dodo Williams and Pastors Curtis and Joyce Levi for their immense love and encouragement.

I also want to appreciate my friends and colleagues for their support and encouragement.

Introduction

The world is engulfed in a sordid fashion of quick business, quick sex, quick fun, quick sleep, fast food, quick marriages, the list is endless.

This fashion has synchronized with the jet age syndrome and has sunk into the age of high-tech which produces goods and services quickly. This syndrome now dictates the fast pace at which things are pursued and it has taken a hold of the human mind.

There is also the craze of the get rich quick which make people insensitive to others and relegate morals to the background. They commit heinous crimes including crimes across the continents. The end justifies the means, they say.

This can also be seen in the quick/fast food industry and its "take away" mentality. It has monumental patronage in spite of the health implications among which are obesity, high blood pressure, diabetes to mention but a few.

Quick fun which is ignited as the world gets into quick manufactures and technological know-how has become the order of the day with youths, teens and young adults over blowing the proportions of HIV/AIDS, STDS, pregnancy, abortion and their attendant health consequences.

Some people have to get quick sleep; and so over dose themselves with sedatives and other drugs to help them relax. This has catapulted the percentage of persons that suffer from insomnia and sleep disorder without realizing that they are gradually drifting into a state of hopeless living and drug dependence.

In quick marriages, the institution of the family which brings stabilizing bonds into the marriage institution is side tracked. These days, young people are sneaking into civic centers and wedding chapels to exchange marital vows without parental consent. It has become a world of wild goose chase and quick fixes.

The Other Side of Desire is a book of cautious optimism and it hinges on the point that bees that have honey in their mouths have stings in their tails. One should be careful, therefore, of people who pretend to be sweet because sweetness is in the honey and not in the bee.

Chapter 1

Microwave Love

A microwave is an electro-magnetic wave of extremely high frequency. Microwave love is a very intense and fiery love that has potentials to burn off quickly due to the fact that it hits the highest height of eroticism too soon. It stems from a desperate craving for sexual excitement for someone. The love as it were, is founded on very fragile grounds and most of the time, cannot stand the test of time.

Microwave love is infatuation. It is a state of being completely carried away by an unreasoned intense love or passion or admiration of someone and it is usually short lived. This is because ecstatic love has potentials to last about thirty months and when the flames burn out; it ebbs and dwindles into thin air. It evaporates; leaving bitter memories, sour tastes and unspeakable resentment of the other person that beats the imagination. Infatuation is characterized by unrealistic expectations of blissful passion without equal growth in the relationship. There is usually no commitment or reciprocated love in infatuation making it a state when someone or something is desperately desired and most times, unattainable.

True love is reciprocated, while infatuation is not mutual. Infatuation comes with feelings of panic, uncertainty, feverish excitement, lust, impatience and lack of concentration. It brings a lot of wear and tear on the body and on the emotions setting the mind ablaze for the moment. Infatuation comes with a lot of thrill and that may not be real happiness; because most of the time, expectations are monumental and there is a lot of acting out, exaggerated feelings and ideas of the object that is desired.

Irrational romantic sentiments stir up a sexually arousing hormone called oxytocin which sometimes overrides the brain activity that governs logical reasoning. Infatuation is like "chemistry" and it is far from real love. It is always good to be truthful to yourself; so that you do not get hurt in the process of giving or receiving love. Giving and receiving love is a doing performance that is tasking to the mind and the body; hence, cautious optimism should be exercised to avoid unnecessary waste of time and emotions. It is necessary that you identify if a relationship is guided by lust, infatuation or love at the onset. This is the greatest justice one can do to oneself, because the pain and drudgery of unfulfilled loving is a canker worm that eats up the beauty of life and living; and this could cause resentment towards the whole idea of loving and being loved for the rest of one's life. Intense pain from loving can be very distasteful and can cause a withholding of love and affection even when the right person comes by.

Infatuation is usually physical and there is a quick urge to consummate love with sex; while real love takes time to grow and is much more enduring than lust or infatuation. Real love can be perceived most of the time. It is a great life experience. It is refreshing and nourishing to the soul and it unfolds in unspeakable grandeur, spiced and garnished with thrills that are unimaginable. Real love is attainable and it speaks even in silence.

In a relationship founded on lust and infatuation, you may not feel good or the same after moments of intimacy with the other person. Repulsing feelings could rear their ugly heads soon after sexual activity. You can identify infatuation easily when someone who claims he loves you, is not excited or willing to talk with you or make eye contact; while lust can be identified if you shift your "love" so easily from one person to another.

Some people enjoy flirting and teasing; and they do not care of the distasteful ripple effects on others. Infatuation is an absorbing and consuming passion. It is sometimes a foolish attraction for someone and it is usually short lived. It is not an ingredient for a long lasting relationship. This is the basis of most traumatic relationships the world over. People are falling in love in night clubs and getting married soon after meeting one another. Many are jumping into bed to get to the heights of sexual experiences soon after their first meeting; sometimes it is after a lunch or dinner date; or a beach outing. Most of the time, emotions burn out as quickly as it was kindled; hence some form of self-control is required; so as to avoid emotional tides and upheavals.

Lust is usually characterized by short physical/emotional relationships because it is an intense sexual desire – an uncontrolled sexual appetite. Lust comes with an insatiable sexual appetite because of the continuous search for thrills and diverse sexual experiences. Sex maniacs endlessly desire these thrills for brief relationships that easily fade away into oblivion. Sex maniacs usually do not have need for long lasting relationship ties; they are ever so eager to move on to the next sex partner.

Identifying lust or infatuation can be assisted when you are away or apart from the other person, and you do not care or miss that person or you are attracted to other people. When lust has been identified, try disengaging from that relationship because it will not survive the test of time. It will cause more harm than envisaged and could cause distasteful memories. Lust is destructive and it often portrays the interest of one person. Lust is unbelievably transient and it is better viewed as a waste of emotions that can have health implications.

There is great contrast between love and lust. True love is neither physical nor romantic; it takes its time to grow, consolidating with time. It comes with reciprocity and a very assuring feeling, while lust rushes and becomes full bloom quickly. Lust is either a sexual or very greedy feeling. While love is more of a secure and content filled feeling which we get through mutual feelings. Lust is more of an inordinate selfishness to possess and lacks depth of purpose. Lust ignores moral principles, after being gratified, has potentials to hurt others because it is a superficial feeling. Love is kind, considerate, caring, giving, thoughtful, understanding, while lust is a temporary craving and more of a greedy desire. Lust is selfish and it is often associated with certain addictions. When a relationship is based on lust, it is fickle and could fizzle out in a moment.

You should be able to sort out through your emotions to honestly tell yourself whether it is love or lust that you are feeling for someone and this will guide you in decision making. You have to work with your feelings, your emotions and your heart in order to feel or get to experience the real, pure, intense love and affection for someone you know you want to be with; and this does not happen in a day.

What feels like love may be mere physical attraction which is a very fragile foundation for a long time relationship. This is the reason people fall in love quickly and also out of love quickly; thereby finding themselves in serial and concurrent relationships. Relationships that are likely to lead to marriage will have these ingredients - trust, respect, caring, commitment, shared interests and reciprocated love.

Chapter 2

Shattered Dreams

Senseless loving can lead to shattered dreams. The human being is most complex and unpredictable even in issues of loving and commitment. Shattered dreams could occur when you get caught up in uncontrollable emotions towards the object of your love. In loving, sometimes "foolish things" are said and done. You drift into a helpless and hopeless situation where you can't help but loving someone.

You stay suspended in your unfathomable dreams sailing through the galaxies, fantasizing in helpless and pitiful emotions.

You are caught in emotions where you endlessly long for the arms of the one you love to wrap around you. You are lost in your imagination figuring and desiring that embrace that may never come. You stay awake all night long in painful and devastating emotions dreaming, fantasizing and longing for that caress, that voice, that phone call, that mail that may never come.

You wake up every morning in hopeful wonder of the possible realization of your dreams. Sound sleep becomes elusive and getting out of bed becomes even more difficult because you are lost in hopeless desire; pondering when you will lay hold on the object of your dreams. In silent storm, your heart weeps and you wonder how long it will take to behold the object of your dreams. Life becomes a lonely place and living becomes a painful existence. Entangled in a messy web, you have no clue how long the pains will last and when you will get out of the mesh. You gaze at day light sometimes aimlessly and wish for nightfall. At nightfall, you hope for the cock crow at dawn.

The tears roll uncontrollably down your sober cheeks; your countenance become pallid. You are speechless for moments untold and your lips become dumb and chapped and you drift into a silent and lonely world. You alone hear your own heartbeats. Your eyes fixed on the ceiling and the encasing walls, piercing through to the other side of the divide.

Your blood chill and coagulate during the cold evenings and the midnight hours. The winter seasons become dreadful due to the envisaged solitude. You dream for the warm spring nights when you can hear the singing birds and the rain drops again; when you can see the flowers budding in beautiful colors. You can't wait for the warm summer nights when mother nature will be warm and friendly, in the lonely moments as you wait for favorable responses from the one you love, the one you long for, the one that has held your heart captive for a while or for so long. You feel crushed, worthless and lonely in a world with a beehive of activities.

Sound reasoning eludes you because you are lost in uncertainty of the perhaps impossible expectations and the yearnings of your heart. Your wanton, mundane and unrealistic desires reap your heart sore and that blood pumping machine, the heart is bleeding for love, for warmth and for fulfillment.

Your yawns turn to painful gasps for love, for a cuddle, for a touch from the only one that make the difference, the one that can restore the smile again to those chapped and bleeding lips. In captivity, you wait spellbound and the days roll into weeks, and the weeks into months and the months into perhaps years of hurting emotions.

Perhaps, you catch glimpses of your heart's most wanted object; but you are constantly visited by a romantic rejection. You drift into self-denial waiting for that romantic acceptance. Sweet sleep eludes you and you remain in the realm of unattainable ambition waiting for a "good day".

As your eyes pop open in the midnight hours, feverish chills envelop you, your sighs become heavy, and your hands tremble for a loving feel, for a loving touch and for reciprocation. You long for the meeting of the two hearts in blissful accord and it is all misery, piercing the fabrics of your being. As the tears flow, psychological relief comes and the suspense becomes bearable pain. Painful reality of the situation comes knocking at the doors of your aching heart ever so frequently.

Soberness visits you as the days go by for time could heal the aching heart; and you can see and hear clearly again.

Unreachable and unattainable becomes the painful verdict and you are tripping from the mountain tops, through the clefts for a hopeless crash. Your emotions tumble from the hill tops to the valley and it is all rubble. Detestable rubbles rumpling your ego and your being for a moment or forever! You dare to pick the bits and pieces of life again, starring at the horizon for meaning and substance of life, of love and loving.

Chapter

3

Even With Flowers

It was the Christmas season and Cherry was all over the malls and shopping centers in Chicago for freaky buys. She had saved for this season and she shopped lavishly for gifts for relations and friends. She had taken time off work with a determination to give herself the best of the season. The season of Christmas is a season that sees the world agog with extraordinary good will and celebrations.

Cherry travelled to the Liverpool sea port in England for the best shoe buys; and she satisfied herself with assorted colors of shoes. She travelled to Paris for the designer dresses where she assembled gorgeous pant suits and evening gowns with exquisite hand bags. She also made a good collection of wears and accessories for crazy party nights of the season. She was poised for a sweet Christmas celebration with a couple of friends.

Cherry and her friends, Natalie and Sandra had planned a catalogue of events for elated and unforgettable celebrations. They planned a trip to Las Vegas via Los Angeles to see the bright Christmas lights along with the dance and theatrical ensembles that Las Vegas is famous for. Cherry had heard so much about Las Vegas and she desired to be there at Christmas.

It was a costly preparation that took her globe-trotting for the craziest fashions. The trip to Las Vegas would cost so much; because of the hotel suites and high costs of entertainment shows. Cherry was to do the trip with her friends Nicole and Sandra. Nicole, Sandra and Cherry were getting ready for a fun trip of their lives; where they intended to have crazy nights and dinner dancing in the coziest of places. They surfed the web for the relaxation spots and where they could also resort to for in-door games because of the cold Christmas season. The friends looked forward with delightful expectations of the trip.

Nicole had joined Cherry on the trip to Paris for high fashion collections; so that they will look exquisite and well put together for the various events they intend to have in Las Vegas. It will be a good thing to take a four day vacation to Las Vegas Cherry, Nicole and Sandra would utter from time to time. They needed a break from the usual routine of work and school in Chicago. They wanted to have a peep into the bright city life of Las Vegas. They wanted another experience, a fun time with diverse people.

Chicago is usually cold and snowy at this time with harsh weather conditions. Sandra did not go out of state for her shopping sprees but had the best from the trendy shops in and around Chicago. They scheduled a first class flight for the round trip via Los Angeles; and were getting their travelling bags ready for the historic trip. They looked forward to seeing the bright evening lights of a place tourists and lovers visit for unusual experiences. They had disengaged from every family event for Christmas; so their friends and families knew of the proposed trip to Las Vegas. They also looked forward to meeting new friends and collecting souvenirs for friends and family at home. It was delightsome preparation and they couldn't wait for the day they had planned to make a brief stop in Los Angeles and take a peek into the hustling city for one day.

Cherry, arrived the mall and shopped all day and became weary. It was a physical exercise that saw her sweating even under the cool autumn weather. She looked out for a place where she could have a mid-day snack with some ice creams and cold drinks. She sat comfortably at the Vintage Restaurant where she treated herself to a sumptuous snack. As she tried to settle her bill, she heard a voice from the table on her side saying "I can help with that." With a smile, Cherry acknowledged the offer and Frank settled the bill with enthusiasm. She exchanged pleasantries with Frank and they got talking for about 30 minutes. Cherry felt good talking with Frank because she had been lonesome for many years and those were the reasons she tried to get away from Chicago at Christmas.

Incidentally, she suffered a heart break a few years ago. She had dated Randy for several years and looking forward to the nuptials; but got the shock of her life when Randy eloped with a pretty brunette from the Canary Islands. Cherry was devastated; and was trying to pick up the bits and pieces of her life at this time. She was elated with the chat and felt quite comfortable with the stranger. Frank, getting positive responses felt good and continued with the conversation.

Frank was just recovering from a break up with Katie; his girlfriend of many years. He was actually on a talk therapy having conversation with Cherry. His doctors had prescribed "talk therapy" as a way of getting his mind off the disturbing thoughts of Katie. He loved Katie with a passion; but they had irreconcilable differences that made the break up inevitable. Undoubtedly, finding a new friend thrilled Frank beyond measure and he desired to see Cherry again.

At the restaurant, they decided to taste some wines before parting for the day. It was warm interactions and Cherry longed for a new friend in Frank; someone to talk with for she had been secluded for a while after her break-up with Randy some years ago. Her planned trip at Christmas to Las Vegas with Nicole and Sandra was another health therapy to help relax her nerve battered nerves and her aching heart. She hadn't had a date in many years and had led a sedentary life, apparently recovering from the heartbreak.

Can we have a date at the weekend? Frank proposed. Cherry felt good going on a date to break the monotony of seclusion and single life. Frank and Cherry looked forward for the date and counted the days as they went by. Frank looked good with trendy features and a deep voice. He was clean shaven with cute side buds and was wearing a brown coat with gorgeous men's boots while Cherry was wearing a doily-esque dress with a winter jacket to protect her from the icy cold.

It was one week to Christmas and Cherry got herself ready for the date. It was a cold evening and she looked forward to meeting Frank again for a pleasurable and eventful night out. They had talked a lot on the telephone and sent loving emails to each other. They were both prepared to have a sweet evening. Frank healing from a recently broken relationship felt that a night out will be quite soothing.

Frank arrived at Cherry's with a bunch of sweet smelling flowers for the date. They were multi colored fresh flowers that was a delightful surprise to Cherry. As Frank presented the flowers to his new found friend, his eyes pierced through the watery blue eyes of Cherry and they were locked in a warm hug. She looked regal and beautiful in a royal blue dress. It was excitements as Frank opened the doors of his posh Lexus car and Cherry was elated as she took her sit for a Lexus ride to Venus Clubs.

They had delightful moments and Frank was profuse over Cherry. Cherry found Frank irresistible. Her eyes dilated with great delight as they did some gigs on the dance floor. Would you be mine? Frank asked Cherry. Cherry responded in the affirmative. What would your week be like? Can we have dinner on Christmas Eve at the Fountain Hotel? Cherry retorted and informed Frank of her intended Christmas trip to Las Vegas with her friends Nicole and Sandra.

Frank assured Cherry of an exciting Christmas celebration in Chicago. Frank wanted company for Christmas for he dreaded the idea of being alone at the festive season. He unfolded an enticing itinerary of events that would bring great delight to their new found friendship. Frank's proposals were irresistible and Cherry remembered Nicole and Sandra for a brief moment.

Caught between two worlds, Cherry remembered the sweet fragrance of the flowers Frank gave her earlier in the evening. The flower was decorated with multi colored ribbons and had a bewitching aroma. No one had ever given her a gift of flowers and she was totally mesmerized. It was sweet moments with Frank that evening at the Venus Clubs; it was love at first sight as they flirted with each other. It was a refreshing Lexus drive back to Cherry's and as Frank gave Cherry the parting kiss, Cherry affirmed to Frank that she would cancel her proposed fun trip to Las Vegas.

I met Frank and we will be spending Christmas together at the Fountain Hotels on Christmas Eve, Cherry informed Nicole and Sandra the next day. Nicole and Sandra remained speechless for a moment. It was broken dreams of their long awaited trip to Las Vegas. The trip won't be the same without you they pleaded with Cherry. My heart melted for Frank as he gave me flowers for our first date Cherry explained to Nicole and Sandra. I want to see him again and spend quality time with him at Christmas as he requested. Continuing, Cherry informed that she wanted to fill the void in his life. In a couple of days, Nicole and Sandra boarded the flight to Las Vegas via Los Angeles. Cherry drove them to the airport and bade them good bye.

Frank would make several calls to Cherry in the course of the day and they both looked forward to their date on Christmas Eve. Frank was at the florist that morning and paid for a home delivery of choice flowers to Cherry. Cherry heard the sound of a van pull up on her drive way and then the gentle knock. It was home delivery from a florist shop. It was a tantalizing bunch of fresh flowers again; adorned with "Merry Christmas" tags. It was awesome and bewitching to look at. It had an amazing softness and fragrance. Cherry cuddled the flowers with amazing delicateness and was lost in loving thoughts of Frank for the rest of the day. She laid in the couch of her cozy living room speechless, admiring the flowers and smelling the sweet fragrance intermittently.

At evening Frank was at Cherry's with a basket of Christmas gifts containing choice perfumes and lingerie. Frank had on a fine tuxedo suit and Cherry wore a colorful azzadine gown suitable for a cold evening. They had great dinner and dancing. They had treated themselves to blues and jazzy music and they were in close hug most of the time. At about 11pm, their eyes twinkled with desire for each other. They needed a cozy environment to be by themselves, separated from a busy world. They felt sweet sensations run through their bodies and could not wait for another date to consummate their relationship. As they felt the continuous torrent of raging hormones, they agreed to relax in each other's arms for the night and have a feel of utopia. Fountain Hotels is known for beautiful "get away" suites.

They checked into the radiant suites of the Fountain Hotels and it was gracious moments all night long. Cherry thanked Frank for the gift of flowers as she chuckled and knuckled in his arms. They were lost in sweet romance, having sexual experiences; and they attained utopic heights many times. Whispers of love filled the cozy blue lit room of their hotel suite. They retired in sweet repose and had thrilling and gracious moments.

As their eyes popped open, it was Christmas morning as they remained hurdled and cuddled up in their exquisite hotel room. It was romance on Christmas morning. It was ecstatic moments for Cherry. She held onto Frank, unwilling to let him go. Frank kissed her profusely until Cherry was breathless. They had a sumptuous Christmas Day lunch at the Fountain Hotels. As Frank took Cherry to her home that afternoon, they agreed to chat on the phone in the evening. Cherry was engulfed with memories of their second date. She longed for yet another date, for more flowers and another opportunity to be locked in a warm embrace with Frank. They teased themselves on the phone at evening time and agreed to have yet another date on New Year's Eve. Frank had promised Cherry a lavish evening to welcome the New Year.

Frank received a call at midweek from his erstwhile lover, Katie. Frank and Katie had broken up at summer time and Katie wanted a "come back." Frank had loved Katie for several years and as Katie pleaded for his love again, Frank promised to see Katie on New Year's Eve. Katie would be flying into Chicago from New York to spend the New Year season with Frank. Frank stopped calling Cherry; because he was not going to see her again. Kate had come back into his life and Frank was giving her a warm welcome into the secret sanctuary of his heart and to be with her for a life time. Kate looked forward for the re-union, for romantic and fulfilling moments with Frank; hopeful that their differences will be sorted out. It was great expectations as Kate flew into Chicago just before the New Year.

Meanwhile, Cherry would wait for Frank's calls unending. She made several frantic calls to Frank and he would not pick her calls anymore. It became pensive and gruesome moments for Cherry as she waited for flowers from Frank for the New Year's Eve. She waited for the ecstatic date Frank had promised. She gazed into the horizon dumbfounded as she waited for his call and for that knock on the door. It was a cold New Year's Eve. She wondered if she will see Frank again. She longed for the sweet fragrance of fresh flowers. She looked out for the florist; hoping that flowers will be delivered one more time to her home. It was heart break at the dawn of the new day. It was lonely and bewildering as Cherry wept profusely.

Chapter 4

Loneliness

Loneliness is a sad feeling people experience. It is a powerful surge of emptiness and solitude. It can manifest in feelings of abandonment, rejection, depression, insecurity, anxiety, resentment, meaninglessness etc. If these feelings are prolonged, they may become debilitating and prevent the affected individual from developing healthy relationships and life styles. Loneliness is a cankerworm that eats deeply into the fabrics of the human mind.

People are alone through circumstances or choice. If the individual is convinced he or she is unlovable, this may increase the experience of suffering and the likelihood of avoiding social contact. Low self-esteem will often trigger the social disconnection which can also lead to loneliness. The lack of friendship relations during childhood or adolescence are causes of loneliness, depression and sometimes celibacy. Loneliness can also be a sign of other social and psychological problems such as chronic depression.

Loneliness does not necessarily mean being alone; because you can feel lonely when you are in a class with 300 other students or in a party or football game with hundreds of screaming spectators. Loneliness is a painful awareness that you are not feeling connected to others and important needs are not being met. Loneliness is when there is no one with whom to share your personal concerns and experiences and you appear to be on a lonely journey of life.

Some people combat the issue of loneliness with pet ownership. Pet ownership is more prevalent in western societies. According to the Centers for Disease Control and Prevention, there is a number of health benefits associated with pet ownership. Companionship is essentially what the animal provides and having a pet is associated with lowered blood pressure and decreased levels of cholesterol. Human connections for purposes of conversations, intimacy and sharing are, however, largely preferred.

Loneliness evokes feelings that one is socially inadequate and this may cause someone to feel that there is something wrong. Loneliness can occur in heavily populated cities and people may feel utterly alone or totally cut off even when surrounded by throngs of people. In a crowd, when there is no deep interaction, it can ignite also feelings of loneliness. It is not the quantity of contacts, but the quality of the contacts that are the determining factors of this social milieu. A lot of people in the society are lonely and they need a change of attitude, demeanor, carriage and facial appearance which may attract others to them.

Loneliness is prevalent in modern days with the society witnessing increase in divorce rates which signifies that families are no more as stable as they used to be. Some married couples are as lonely as if they were eternally single due to irreconcilable marital issues. The breakdown of family ties sadly strengthens the concept of individualism. About 100 years ago, families still bonded together and there were fewer divorces. The trend has changed drastically all over the world with the disintegration of the family institution. In a place like the United States alone, the statistics is that a quarter of the United States population lived alone in 1998 and people are having fewer and fewer friends and confidants.

There is a strange paradox that loneliness can occur within marriages or similar close relationships where there is anger, resentment or where love cannot be given or received. This represents communication breakdown and it takes its ugly toll on relationships and marriages. Loneliness can also be initiated by loss of a loved one. In this case, loneliness is still an issue to deal with even when one is in a company of people. Socially disruptive events and relocating from a certain geographical area can cause loneliness as well. Learning to cope with changes in life patterns and circumstances is essential in overcoming loneliness.

Feeling lonely can make you sick, affect the genes or lure you into doing drugs and high alcohol and tobacco consumption. There is a relationship between social experiences and physical health. The feeling of isolation and loneliness is a painful emotional state for people and can surely lead to ill health both physically and mentally.

The elderly singles who have very little activity and socialization are a serious case in point in that they are more prone to depressive moods caused by lonely feelings. At this stage, friendships and family ties may not be readily available since people they are dependent on may be busy at work places or engaged with many social events or involved with their own immediate families. Chronic loneliness is a serious life-threatening condition with an increased risk of stroke, cardiovascular diseases, cancer, depression, suicide etc.

Tips For Overcoming Loneliness

1. For singles who are feeling the pangs of loneliness, when visiting Restaurants or Banquet Halls, try inviting someone to go along with you; so that you do not just ask for **a "Table For One"** which makes you eat alone and keeps you in your own little world; but ask for Table for two or three as the case may be- the more, the merrier.

2. Call and get together with people as often as possible. Telephoning is a good form of social contact. Try being a member of a group because it is good for social identity which humans as

social beings need for good psychological health. Consider fellowships with those of your faith. Most religious institutions have some sort of regular fellowships and activities. This will ease feelings of loneliness.

3. Get involved in activities, hobbies, arts or cultural events where you will meet people; people who can brighten your mood. But be careful here so that cults do not find you vulnerable.

4. Embark on some volunteer or community work to fill up your free moments and keep you busy and possibly forming social relationships. Helping others will boost your self-esteem and you feel good about yourself.

5. With the advent of the internet which reduces the world to a global village, find individuals or groups on line to keep busy. Online chats could help.

6. When feeling lonely, do something like take a walk, ride your bike, play a game, listen to music, watch a favorite television show, take yourself out on a date to a good restaurant, a movie etc.

7. Read literature and go to the museums, theatres, dances or window shopping.

1. Consider getting a Pet. Animals can make good companions. Walking a dog can also be a great way of meeting other people and it has also been known in medical sciences to reduce cholesterol and high blood pressure.

1. Learn to smile and say "hello" and initiate short conversations with people.

2. Do not spend your time eating and drinking endlessly or worrying about your problems.

3. Do not judge people on the basis of your past experience. Give new people you meet a chance and try to get to know them. Learn to admire and accept the individual differences in people.

4. Because stress is a part of human existence, affiliations and social interactions should be sought to combat consequences of loneliness because loneliness could heighten the effects of stress on the human mind and body.

5. Because each individual is unique, perceive yourself in a positive way, like yourself and be happy. You have a right to be happy; live a life of optimism. If, however, you have a persistent feeling of loneliness, please seek medical help to avoid depression and suicidal thoughts.

Chapter 5

Loving The Wrong Person

Loving is the art of showing love or giving love or feeling love. It is being warmly affectionate towards someone. It is a feeling of a warm personal attachment or deep affection. It can also mean sexual passion or desire. It is a profoundly tender feeling that beats human imagination and the origin of love and loving is as long as creation. When the desire is right, loving is a most fulfilling act that keeps a person happy and smiling for the slightest reason.

When someone smiles, early wrinkles are defied; because smiling gives tone to the facial muscles.

Loving the wrong person is an assault to one's emotions. This is a situation that occurs when there has not been enough time to determine if the emotional reactions are mutual. People are usually selfish because, it is all about who they want and not who wants them. The other party could actually respond on the spur of the moment due to certain physical attractions which is the hallmark of lust and infatuation. Loving is a consuming feeling; and people should be a little more careful to guard their heart from being crushed. Loving the wrong person is an uphill task, an excruciating and painful experience.

Jessica got caught in intense passion and wallowed in uncontrollable passion. Jessica met Randy at a Pub. They danced and cuddled like love struck teenagers all night long. Randy was thrilling, intriguing and a prolific dancer. He had won many dancing competitions in the past. Doing the gig on the dancing floor was one of his hallmarks. He is a star of the highest magnitude. Jessica was thrilled beyond measure because Randy was fondly attracted to her and made her his dancing partner all night long. Jessica, a blonde, wore a doily-esque dress and sexy panty hose. She also did cute gyrations on the dance floor making them an attractive couple at the Pub.

It was midnight and the music became bluesy; the gyrations slowed down into intimate close-up dancing. Jessica was mesmerized with the feel of Randy's body because they locked in a passionate hugging position. He had on the Givenchy cologne for men and in a moment, Jessica was lost in his arms speechless. Randy responded on the spur of the moment, giving her gentle caresses. Men being visual creatures, Randy could see that she looked good and had a nice soft body with good girlish curves.

She looked impressive and had a dress sense that would attract any eye. She had large blue piercing eye balls and Randy saw that ever so often, Jessica would fix a gaze at him. Exhibiting a body language suggestive of her desires, Randy, showed a tendency to vacillate. He was single and was still a student of the Performing Arts at the University. He was often invited to shows to exhibit latest dance steps; and this physical activity gave him a healthy physique and smart gait. He was always on tight jeans trousers to bring out the best of dancing steps.

Randy organized high profile music shows and always had seasoned stage presence; exuding professionalism at all times. He made money dancing at night clubs and entertainment centers; and he would also sing from time to time stringing the guitar. He played a variety of songs ranging from jazzy to country music. He was a bluesy crooner at night clubs, a dance and music icon and has a string of admirers.

As they got ready to leave the club, Randy said a mere "thanks for the evening"; and Jessica requested Randy to meet her at the club the next evening. They met as scheduled and she treated Randy to sumptuous refreshments and drinks. Flattering her sensuous body all around him, Randy kissed her profusely with an irresistible candor. They got onto the dance floor again.

Jessica wore a trendy little blouse that displayed too much cleavage with a lot of her "goods" hanging out. This embarrassed Randy who would have been much more comfortable without the undue exposure of her sensitive parts. It was fun as usual as Randy did on the dance floor what he knows how best to do. As they came together to do close-up dancing, Jessica found Randy totally irresistible and she proposed friendship to Randy whispering into his ears. Randy was mute; because he was not mentally and emotionally prepared for a relationship. He felt like getting away but he continued to be polite and respectful so as not to hurt Jessica who was profuse and all over him. They exchanged contact information and as they bade themselves goodbye, Jessica knew that she had fallen in love with Randy. She was overwhelmed with passion and gazed at him with intense desire. It was difficult for her to let Randy go, but he had to leave because the night was far spent.

It was uncertain if Randy will desire a relationship with her, but that was the least of her problems. She was ready to throw caution into the wind and make positive impressions on Randy's heart. She wanted a space in his heart and a romantic acceptance at all cost. As Randy was hopping into his car, she reached to him for a good night kiss and Randy was offish. An icy response it was. "I want you Randy, I'm falling in love with you and I can't help myself", Jessica muttered dejectedly.

She would call Randy ever so often; and Randy avoided many of her calls. Jessica visited the club again hoping to catch sight of Randy; and silently asked Venus to give her success on her search for love. Love she so desperately wanted. Randy was on the dancing floor with Betty; a petite girl from Hollywood who is also a music icon and a stage crooner. Jessica tried getting Randy's attention but Randy was glued to Bettie with a stunning passion. Randy astutely ignored Jessica and did not acknowledge her presence. He paid quality attention to Bettie and refused to be distracted.

Jessica drove back home, disturbed at her unattainable desire and was having painful reflections of the romance between Randy and Bettie. She sobbed profusely, romanticizing and holding desperately onto the nice moments which she previously had with Randy. As she made yet another appearance at the club, she met Randy with Princess who is a tantalizing model with the Peavey Magazine.

Jessica dared a quick chat with Princess and the response was cordial because Princess is pleasantly disposed. "Good evening" Jessica said to Randy. Randy gave Jessica an icy welcome for obvious reasons that he had company - one too many. Princess had an incredible charm as she looked appropriately regal in a green-colored jacket, short skirt, high-heeled shoes and an exquisite green purse. She had on bling and accessories that glittered through the dimly lit club and Randy was all over her.

Jessica was totally devastated at the romantic rejection which she received from Randy. She drove home alone, on a lonely road on that cold and icy winter night. It was a lonely night as she tossed and turned all night long on her bed. Sleep eluded her, her rosy cheeks turned pallid, and she felt the winter cold piercing through her bones. Thoughts of Randy engulfed her aching heart and she relived sweet memories of their first meeting.

Chapter

6

Single By Choice

A broader perspective is essential in addressing the issues of singleness. There are a small percentage of people in the entire global population that are singles by their own choices for reasons that are varied and individualized. Man is a very complex being and highly unpredictable. There are instances of deviations from normal societal norms and expectations due to different circumstances. It is important that this be understood; so that judgmental attitudes on singles may be minimized.

For some people, it is not a case of deviation from societal norms but that of total commitment to a life time of service to God and this requires them to be single without having marital relations. In some denominations, it is a fundamental requirement for priests/clergy to be single in order to devote all their time and energy to their holy vocational calling. Most societies are familiar and well disposed towards such persons who have made this ecclesiastical choice.

However, some members of the clergy who have taken the oath of celibacy default seriously in this area as can be evidenced by the numerous law suits and litigations charging them for various sexual offences. It is a pitiful situation which holds out a moral question and further requires self-examination before taking this oath; so as not to bring disrepute to religious institutions.

The truth is that the raging hormones in humans as well as the brain "pleasure centers" make constant demands for gratification in the human body. This could cause some members of the clergy to default by them having and satisfying passionate feelings as the case may be. The consequence of this is falling short on their sworn oaths to a life of celibacy.

Some people take to singleness by choice because they do not want to be encumbered with the responsibilities of marriage and raising children. Some people in this category either decide to be alone and have members of the opposite sex as mere friends or they take to having animals as companions including also other past times and paid jobs.

Women owe it to the feminist movement that women now have more freedom to make choices in their love lives including the choice to remain single. In interpreting and living a life of freedom, care should be taken by both sexes not to get into risky and questionable behaviors. These have potentials for undue exposure to health hazards and bad peers or getting into questionable past times.

It is a known fact that some singles by choice have animals as companions, with undue emotional attachments with these animals. Examples of this man/animal relationship which they have as a result of their choice to remain single are sharing pillows and beds with these animals, hugging and kissing their animals with undue passion which becomes questionable and leaves much to be desired. These practices could raise questions about the mental health status of these singles by choice and there may be need for specialist counsel.

This somewhat misdirected passion with animals is misdirected because by creation, the human brain as it were, has "pleasure centers" that are constantly seeking for pleasure and satisfaction. When these electrifying sensations in man incline towards having animal relationships, it becomes suspicious and indeed unpalatable and may require medical intervention. With a high noticeable increase in these passionate relationships with "companion animals," the world is witnessing many hard-to-cure diseases with origins of these diseases a puzzle to medical researchers and scientists.

Singlehood as a life choice violates cultural norms in most societies and there are more often than not, normative pressures to conform to societal norms and expectations and this is the "hostile" environment that singles by choice live in and this environment isolates their purpose.

Reasons

1. One of the biggest perceived advantages of being single by choice is "independence and autonomy."

2. Some people prefer remaining single because they can have more "fun."

3. Singles by choice rely on peers for support and companionship instead of relying and interacting with spouses.

4. Some people remain single for fear of commitment and emotional heart breaks as the case may be.

5. Some people remain single for fear of domestic violence and brutalities experienced by other close members of family and friends. So they lead their lives "saying better to be single and happy than being married and crushed".

6. Divorce and prolonged years of conflict between parents can have a negative effect on young adults' perceptions of marriage.

7. People with physical or emotional problems are more likely to remain single longer or not marry in their lifetime.

Being dispassionate and broadening the scope of this topic under exposition, being single presents an opportunity to grow as a person, to appreciate oneself and one's idiosyncrasies. It could present a time to make someone a force to be reckoned with in the academia, in career, in developing one's spirituality, in giving time for research and community service etc.

Things that singles by choice may enjoy are the diligent use of their time which may help them in making more realistic projections of attainable goals. Without spousal interferences, they take unilateral decisions in most areas of their lives, could re-decorate their own homes at any time and work with their own time and enjoy also a life free of matrimonial stress and conflicts.

This, being their well-considered choice in the light of their individual circumstances and preferences, coping mechanisms for the life style they have chosen have been developed and plans for their old age and issues concerning their wills when they pass have been articulated.

In the midst of the aforementioned, notwithstanding, there is still social pressure to be married by a certain age in most cultures. Expectedly, negative judgmental attitudes of society are constantly issues that single by choice adults face in their work places and day to day living in the society.

Chapter

7

Hiv/aids And Health Implications

Spontaneous relationships and risky sexual behaviors as well as unprotected sex are factors that cause the most dreaded disease the world may ever know. The HIV/AIDS crisis poses one the greatest challenges ever faced by man. It threatens our health, disrupts families, destabilizes workforces and businesses and destroys communities.

HIV/AIDS has quickly become one of the most serious health and development problems facing the world today and the frightening statistics show clearly that man's efforts to combat AIDS have so far been both too little too late. Over 34 million people are currently infected with HIV, the virus that causes AIDS. No place on earth has been untouched. In 2001 alone, AIDS was responsible for about 3 million deaths and 20 million have died of AIDS since the beginning of the epidemic. By now, deaths due to HIV/AIDS have surpassed the 20 million Europeans killed by the plague epidemic of 1347-1351. Each day, AIDS claims at least 5500 men, women and children, more than double the number killed by malaria. More than 80 percent of AIDS deaths have occurred in Africa.

Globally, an estimated 14,000 people are infected with HIV every day. In Botswana, one third of the population carries HIV and the life expectancy has fallen from 62 years – to 37, entirely as a result of AIDS. This is highly unacceptable. HIV/AIDS must not be allowed to compromise the development gains won through hard economic, social and political struggle. The present trend has to be halted and this can only be achieved by series of initiatives at grassroots levels. HIV/AIDS is not another man's disease. It affects all of us either as infected or affected individuals or our friends or families.

It is necessary, however, to give the medical facts of this disease. As frightening as the picture may look, the future is not irredeemably bleak. We know a lot more about the disease than we did in the past and the future does not have to be like the past. We know now that HIV cannot be transmitted through casual contact. That means that a person cannot become infected with HIV from a handshake, a sneeze, a hug, or from sharing cups and dishes, tools, telephones, computer keyboards, bathroom facilities or drinking fountains. You cannot simply "catch" HIV from air, food, water, insects or animals.

HIV, the virus that causes AIDS, is transmitted in the following ways:

1. By having unprotected sexual intercourse (vaginal, anal or oral) with a man or woman who is infected with the virus. This route accounts for 80% of infections today.

2. By sharing needles or syringes with someone who is infected with the virus

3. From an HIV-infected woman to her child during pregnancy of childbirth or in rare cases, through

breastfeeding (this risk can be reduced significantly with new drug therapies)

4. By receiving HIV-infected blood, blood products, plasma or transplanted tissues or organs.

5. By blood to blood contact with a person infected with HIV when no physical barrier such as vinyl or latex gloves are used.

People should exercise caution in having sexual relations. Intimacy is the height of erotic feelings and it should be done safely and discreetly. The fact is that during sexual intercourse, the couple is plugging into a network of all previous sexual partners and an already infected partner will contaminate the other person. The price for pleasure could be a very costly and life threatening and this call for extreme care and thoughtfulness. Taking a careless plunge into the arms of a stranger is wary. Care-free dating sprees, quick sex and swapping should be avoided. Self-control is needed and medical information of partners should primarily be sought before intimacy.

HIV/AIDS in not only a medical or social problem, it is also a concern for businesses. Young people who are tomorrows' business leaders should have this information so in the future they will enforce programs like the role of businesses in disease prevention and health promotion. This promotion had in the past been the responsibility of public health officials, medical doctors, nurses and other health professionals. This is fundamental because HIV/AIDS has become an epidemic and a major global concern.

HIV/AIDS presents a major obstacle in peaceful co-existence in families, economic growth and even stability in places of work. Without a healthy society and workforce, the potentials and steady growth of society is seriously affected. The cost of doing nothing about AIDS far surpasses the cost of fighting it at a later time. In business places for instance, there are financial implications for training new hires to replace employees lost to the HIV/AIDS epidemic.

Young people who take on jobs or apprentice engagements as laboratory workers, health care workers and persons dealing with hospital waste products, emergency medical response personnel and any other occupation where there is a possibility of exposure to blood. Among the hazards to which these persons may be exposed are syringe needle injuries and other skin-piercing accidents and splashing into the eyes while they are administering treatment or otherwise performing their duties.

AIDS primarily kills young and middle-aged adults during their reproductive and most productive years. A fundamental feature of AIDS is that its impact is subtle, gradual, long term, and complex. The costs associated with HIV illness have undoubtedly become a social responsibility as they affect all parts of our society, from our community to our workplaces. The joint response of schools, families, and businesses to this cancerous problem is, hereby, being advocated.

Chapter 8

Single Parenthood

Frivolous sexual activities, serial marriages, high rate of divorce are factors that cause the phenomenon of single parenthood. A devastating and sore point is that more and more teenagers are becoming single parents. Older adults who become single parents are better able to cope with this highly demanding social milieu than the younger persons. A single parent is a parent who cares for one or more children without the assistance of another parent in the home. The term single parent is also known as "sole parent" or "lone parent". One may become a single parent through divorce, adoption, extramarital pregnancy or by an unforeseeable occurrence such as abandonment or death of the other parent.

Single parenting is a totally different world from regular parenting (households with a father and a mother). There is need to be adjusted to the activities that are expected from both parents. A single father may be faced with the need to provide nurturing, love and care to their children; a task which women are good at. There is a need for both parents to be involved in child rearing; for purposes of emotional and physical support in the assiduous task. Single parenting surely present challenges to the offspring as well as the parent. Some of these challenges are unforeseen most of the time. Every effort should be made to avert the circumstances that have the potentials to make one a single parent.

It is difficult today to be a parent and even more difficult to be a single parent. The fact that this can be an enormous task cannot be overemphasized. Single parenting can be overwhelming which compels one to learn parenting skills necessary to do a good job. It may appear as having two jobs at once. Managing the household, taking kids to school, for clinical checks and trying to keep up with many hours of work are responsibilities of parents. This is usually an overwhelming responsibility and sometimes single parents are compelled to establish "work from home businesses." This could limit their potentials and networking in an ever challenging business landscape that the world is witnessing at the moment.

Some people also become single parents by choice for reasons varied and individualized. The women who decide by choice to be single parents tend to be educated, career women and most times they are over 35 years. Children born to such "choice mothers" may not face problems of poverty, housing, education etc. Choice mothers and children may face other problems of loneliness, depression and other emotional situations. A small number of men also decide to be "choice fathers." A circumstance that may influence this choice is failed expectations in previous relationships.

There is a growing trend among all adult women to have children regardless of their marital status. In 2007 alone, about 40% of births were to unwed mothers. Supporting this trend is the established fact that most single parents are females. Population survey has it that in 2006 in the United States, 10.4 million women were single parents living with their children while 2.5 million were single father families.

In 2001 in Australia, 31% of babies born in Australia were born to unmarried mothers. In the United Kingdom in the year 2005, there were 5.9 million single parents.

There is a school of thought that supports the fact that this rising phenomenon contributes significantly to societal ills. Human societies are constantly faced with issues of social menace and social malaise. This has caused great concern to governments and families because of the grave dangers that are inevitable consequences. In some societies, there are established institutions to address these issues and to keep them from escalating.

The fear is that children from single parent families may not have adequate control and supervision that is required in the period of growing up; especially during personality and character formation. Submission to peer pressure and risky adventures are the characteristics of children that are not adequately monitored. Juvenile delinquency, truancy, bullying and school absenteeism are more likely to be associated with children that are under supervised. This scenario, notwithstanding, most children from single parent families do well and the determining factors are the parent's educational level, age, occupation, income and support networks of friends and family.

Single parenthood is a stage of life and some re-marry and then form a step family. There is usually no guarantee that the marriages will be successful; because sometimes, unknowingly, the emotional baggage of the past is carried into the new relationship. Sour past experiences become easy reference points most of the time, thereby, putting pressure on the new relationship. This can cause irritability on the partners and the once romantic relationship begins to experience wear and tear. Suspicion, insecurity and high expectations begin to cause friction and the hydra headed problems could lead to unforeseen separation or divorce and the persons become regrettably single parents again.

The tortuous cycle continues; hence uneventful relationships abound. The issues and problems of single parenthood are individualized and diverse and as undesirable as it sounds, it has become a social phenomenon to be reckoned with at this age and time. Single parenthood presents a situation where one of the parents is alone and has the cumbersome responsibility of making unilateral decisions and being alone most of the time. With this situation, the parent discusses financial and family concerns with the children which in couple families, such discussions would take place between the parents.

This arises when the single parent is overwhelmed with issues of running the household. It is an obvious burden and addition most of the time to growing children to come to the round table and sit in concert with one of their parents to make decisions. This is an early and cumbersome responsibility on children and sometimes children find themselves growing up rapidly sorting out adult problems which by their age they cannot appropriately handle. It is best to let children be children, while the single parent finds solutions and comfort elsewhere. It is good to understand these details; so that informed decisions will be made by couples who intend to separate or divorce.

There is tremendous effect on the actors involved in this social circumstance of single parenthood. It is an established fact that it is the children who pay the price. If this situation has been caused by the death of one of the parents, the children have emotional problems which the "Father's Day" or "Mother's Day" presents. They have no one to send that Christmas or Easter or Happy Birthday card to. That's a vacuum right there and they have to deal with it for the rest of their lives.

Effects Of Single Parenthood

1. Single parent families are at a higher risk of poverty than families where both parents are available. This tends to make children of single parents fend for themselves or stray away with the crowd in search of "green pastures".

2. In many cases, single mothers have poorer health than coupled mothers.

3. Children of single parents are more likely to have emotional and behavioral problems like attempting or committing suicide, truancy, gang action tendencies.

4. Overwhelming stress on single pregnant mothers. The much needed emotional support which will make them "happy and healthy mothers" is lacking and this is a very depressing state for both young and

5. older mothers.

6. Presents a probable higher rate of puerperal psychosis in post-delivery conditions of single pregnant mothers. This is because they are left

alone to handle chores and fend for themselves and baby at a most delicate period when they need nurturing and support themselves.

7. It presents children with the responsibility of looking after themselves at an earlier age or as the case may be. Sometimes, children become depressed and develop mental health problems and identity problems.

Coping Tips

Fundamentally, two parents' households are better and present a better environment to raise children. However, in the event that this is inevitable; instead of drifting into depression and anxiety, these are some coping tips:

1. Have a positive attitude and cling to the fact that single parenting presents a situation of less conflict in the home and there is more independence in decision making and in other areas of life.

2. Focus on success, set goals and get your priorities right. Be hopeful and positive of new things to happen and look forward to meeting someone new that will bring a new dimension to your life.

3. Establish clear boundaries that you are the boss at home and that the children are not peers or equal partners and bring order to the home by instilling some forms of discipline. Do not let children manipulate you and be in control as much as possible.

4. Do not be overwhelmed with chores at home, delegate tasks and chores to the children. They have youthful energy to cope with the demands of household chores and encourage them to spend the energy purposefully.

5. Have family meetings as often as you can and listen to the input of the children. This improves communication and further allows for early intervention in problem areas. Talking and listening to your children will break down dividing walls and you will get to know them better.

6. Make friends quickly and ask understanding families for help. Develop a network of reliable and effective relationships that can assist in times of emergencies. This will make you feel better mentally and physically too. It douses the spirit of lonesomeness.

7. Provide a nurturing environment within the limits of your income and be sufficiently loving and caring to them. Build them up and not put them down so that they can grow up and have stable personalities. This will also help them not to carry baggage into future lives and relationships.

8. Do not treat your child as a peer and do not turn to your child for emotional support by confiding in him/her. Allow children to be children and find other adults for companionship and emotional support.

9. When your kids are howling at each other, don't get agitated or depressed; you can try praying for divine intervention to see them through growing up.

10. Pray for the right person to come into your life, look good, be happy, eat well and have a good night's sleep as much as you can. Avoid sedatives as much as you can; so that you don't develop insomnia or sleep problems.

11. If you are feeling overwhelmed, anxious, depressed, seek therapeutic or medical help.

While advising that the rate of single parenthood be kept considerably low, it is necessary at this point to advise that families, governments and communities should be enlightened on the tremendous stress of this condition on single pregnant mothers. There are mental health conditions associated with stress in pregnancy and post-delivery conditions. This is known as puerperal psychosis and can lead to death and hospitalization of the mother.

Sometimes, single parenthood is a gruesome experience; especially where there are limited finances to cope with the demands of everyday living. There are serious inflationary trends all over the world and living standards are falling for most people. An inadequate finance for a single parent is devastating because it will cause serial problems which may become complicated in due course.

There is a steady decline in traditional families and individualism seems to be the prevailing order. This leaves the single parent to his/her faith and circumstance. This has been influenced by rising literacy rates and globalization with different perspectives emerging in a complex and fast paced world.

There is a growing trend among all adult women to have children regardless of their marital status. In 2007 alone, about 40% of births were to unwed mothers. Supporting this trend is the established fact that most single parents are female. Population survey has it that in 2006 in the United States, 10.4 million women were single parents living with their children while 2.5 million were single father families. In 2001 in Australia, 31% of babies born in Australia were born to unmarried mothers. In the United Kingdom in the year 2005, there were 5.9 million single parents.

Single parenthood presents a situation where one of the parents is alone and with the cumbersome responsibility of making unilateral decisions. With this situation, the parent discusses financial and family concerns with the children which in couple families, such discussions would take place between the parents. It is an obvious addition most of the time to growing children to come to round table and sit in concert with one of their parents to make decisions.

To this effect, there should be more government involvement and support in the areas of provision of food, money, medical care and housing for these single pregnant mothers. These provisions should be institutionalized so as to ameliorate the mental and physical stress of single parenthood. This may go a long way of reducing the incidences of maternal morbidity, maternal mortality, puerperal psychosis, street children, abortion and baby dumping. To this effect, teachers, coaches, family members, friends and neighbors should be extra sensitive and compassionate

Chapter 9

Puzzling

All night long
I lay tossing and turning
Looking for the one my heart loves
I looked for him but could not find him.
I will search for the one my heart loves, everywhere!

Unsatisfied love withers and dies. If two people have too many irreconcilable differences, their love for each other will wither and die; and they will begin to witness a frictions and conflicts in their relationship. When two people have more differences than similarities, love cannot be nourished or sustained. Differences are vehicles of conflict and resentment. The relationship becomes transient with repulsing feelings for each other. This could be a terrible state and it has the potentials to make you "shut down" from continuing in the relationship or marriage or even still from falling in love again.

When your love is lost, you may feel crushed and this takes you into harrowing and puzzling moments and you wonder where things fell apart. Loving someone again may become difficult because of memories of the previous distasteful and unexciting relationship. You feel disillusioned and may come to believe that romantic love is a false ecstatic feeling that takes you to utopic heights only for the moment.

This unpalatable situation comes up when people who fall in love sense the beginning of problems. They know that romantic love can produce great joy and happiness, but with time, they begin to feel more alone and unconsciously drift into a "lonely world" where their erstwhile passionate hearts would cry for help:

Alas, where is my beloved!!!
Oh no!

This can't be
This can't be true
This hurts
Oh my gosh!

Issues of self-doubt and shattered dreams begin to rear their ugly heads. Failed expectations cause you to see the other person in his/her true state. Fault finding, disenchantment, anger, bitterness and cynicism engulf the once romantic relationship. At this point, some lovers or couples separate or remain together in misery. They feel stuck in the relationship because of their children or they try to raise a family in an effort to revive the relationship.

With this scenario, lovers begin to seek for "greener pastures" somewhere else, searching for another sexual experience. Married couples begin to have extra marital affairs and spend more time with their new dates. With a consequent separation or divorce another love affair or relationship begins too quickly. This is due to the fact that an urgent need arises to ease the pain of separation or to reduce the pangs of loneliness and a broken heart. The same cycle of events could start again because sooner than later, people begin to make the same mistakes as in their previous relationships, thereby, leading to serial marriages.

However, the percentages of people who eventually fall in love all over again far out- weigh the percentage that shuts down forever. This is because the stage following the pain of heart break could be a long or flighty one. It is called the healing process. When you recover from the past pains, new love can start because your life is not over yet. Many people fall in love and out of love many times in their life time. This, however, leaves much to be desired. Some people have very strong coping mechanisms to see them through this painful and harrowing process.

The case of Abigail and George was a very sorry one. Abigail met George in high school and they fell head over heels in love with each other. As high school sweet hearts, they had lots of fun during school vacations. They were at the beaches, pubs and sporting events together. George was an athlete who did very well in basketball. He looked forward to being a basketball star. He was about seven feet tall with a strong and tantalizing physique. Abigail was a trendy teenager with great aspirations for academics. They graduated from high school and went into the same college;

so as to keep the romance alive. The coaches of different basketball clubs wooed George offering him great pay and remunerations because he was a very promising athlete.

He excelled in championships and was distinguished on the field as a superstar. George joined one of the clubs and had great fans and wealth. Abigail toured with him to watch her hero do the games and it was lavish and exciting moments with each victory for George and Abigail. George was ascending great heights and they started talking about their future aspirations. They planned to buy a home at summer time and to have a summer wedding which will attract celebrities and members of their families from different parts of the world.

It was great expectations for Abigail who had given her heart to George. She loved George with an incredible passion and would delightfully talk about George with her friends. She was proud that George was taking the front and center pages of the magazines, highly glamorized for his athletic exploits. She looked forward to a celebrity wedding, to highly priced wedding and engagement rings and to a fabulous day which will see herself and her high school sweetheart as man and wife.

Early spring season, about two months to their summer wedding, George during a telephone conversation said, "Abigail, I don't love you anymore". It was a great puzzle to Abigail because all seemed right. Her world came crashing and bewilderment engulfed her as tears ran down her rosy cheeks.

Chapter 10

Tears For Love

Listen to my tears fall,
And how they fall like rain.
The tears burn like acid,
to slowly kill me.
Pain unimaginable.
You made life one whole
You've torn it apart!

Paradoxically, the above poem depicts some of the consequences of a failing love affair. Sometimes we love the wrong people and pay so much for casting pearls to "the dogs".

Suspense, anxiety and fear characterize many love relationships. There is excruciating pain when waiting for the telephone to ring; so that you can hear the voice of your beloved. The rate of your heart beats increase when you have to anxiously wait for the knock on the door or for the car to pull up. During festive occasions you are looking forward to the offer of a cute vacation or for the cards and the flowers to arrive. Sometimes you are kept waiting for the hug, the kisses, the smile, the caresses and cuddles.

Sometimes you are longing for a date with your partner, a candle light dinner somewhere; or a drive around town for sight-seeing and refreshing moments. Sometimes, you are longing for a trip to the sea side, the beach, and the mountain tops fore extraordinary moments. Sometimes, it is the longing for a swimming delight with your partner for a new experience with the world of the marines. Sometimes, it is to go fishing or a sport or visit the beach for the cool sea breeze to soothe the aching nerves and energize the body and soul again which would undoubtedly bring rejuvenation to the relationship.

Fear and anxiety make you trembling for love and sometimes you have to keep a fixed gaze on the drive way to see when your sweetheart will pull up to a warm welcome.

You get into illusions and imaginations of your heart where your beloved is and the possible time of arrival. Your eyes are glued to the ticking clock in elated expectancy.

Sometimes, your love has not returned your calls, your emails or letters. Is everything alright? You seem to wonder and wandering thoughts engulf your bleeding heart. What do I do? You wonder in amazing grief. Grief strong enough to cost you the midnight rest envelopes you. Sleep eludes you and you toss and turn on your cold and lonely bed.

Your heart is bursting, the chills run through you and the visible tears begin to flow like drops of blood from a bleeding heart. Unbearable and crushing moments come in close shave. Spasms of pain engulf you and you no longer hear the singing of the birds or see the beauty of the budding flowers at spring time, and summer sunrays become unbearably scorching.

The fear of the love lost makes your hairs stand and your face pallid. The pupils of your eyes dilate with pain. The tear glands are busy as your eyes bleed with tears continuously and profusely. Tears of anguish, tears for the erstwhile good times that appear forever gone, fear of the unknown future. You remember the candle light dinners, the rosy and the romantic past, the sharing, the elating and exhilarating moments and your heart would sink.

You remember the sweet slumber of the past when sleep was sweet dreams as in a world of peace and tranquility. A world you had a little peep at for a while, when your lover would light up the azures of the skies and how your raging hormones sang for joy. You remember also the exotic places you visited and the gifts and intimate moments you shared. You are left wandering in space and encapsulated in anguish, muttering and sighing for a wasted time of giving and loving.

Where is my heartthrob? What happened? What went wrong and what do I do now? Do I give my love another call or send flowers, cards, emissaries or ask for a chat? You are as it where left stranded at the wonder land; abandoned in the middle of the deep blue sea, in the middle of nowhere.

The days ahead become long discordant days and music tunes no longer harmonize in your ears. When it is morning, you wish it was nighttime! When it is noon, you wish it was the wee hours of the morning! Where is the fragrance of love gone to? You marvel in pitiful silence how to drowse the painful feelings. Living becomes a dilemma and you begin to withdraw into a cocoon to nurse your wounded heart. The stars become dim and the deep blue skies become blurry.

As your eyes pop open at morning, you are glued to your bed unable to do the smart swing of getting out of bed; unable to arise to see the beauty of the new day. What is new about the day when you are at a crossroad, lonely and in a strange world.

Chapter 11

Crazy Love

Sometimes people get into "crazy love" which impacts on the mental health and this could lead to depression, suicide or homicide. "Crazy love" could lead to serious mental health problems if it is not controlled. There are overwhelming media reports of incidences of domestic violence and spousal homicide where one time lovers get into strange behavior and hurt themselves for reasons that are varied and individualized.

When love is reciprocated, it is an exhilarating feeling. It is a strong and overwhelming feeling, an uncontrollable and inexplicable feeling. Loving is a delightful feeling that keeps your heart pumping fresh blood around your system. People die for love as an expression of true love. Loving is a healthy act that, and it is as old as humanity. However, do not expect the other person to give love back to you in exactly the same way as you give it and do not make an "idol" of who you love; so that you do not overwhelm the other person. You may lose your love because of enormous pressure on the relationship and when you idealize the person. Self-control, keeping your emotions under check, and not sounding controlling will give your partner breathing space. Some people suffocate their love with attention -seeking habits and this could diminish love.

Infatuation may be the ripple effect of crazy loving. Infatuation may be true but does not necessarily lead to a lengthy relationship or marriage. This is because infatuation is towards something highly admired and desired but most of the time unattainable. Infatuation is more concerned with physical attributes and desire for sexual gratification. It is usually transient and it is a selfish feeling to satisfy sexual cravings and urges.

There is a difference between love, infatuation and lust. Lust is usually expressed through short, physical and intensely emotional relationships. Lust can easily be identified when your "love" shifts from one person to another. Lust is mostly a physical relationship. Lust is destructive because it has implications of frivolity and health hazards. Some people can hurt the object of their love because they are lustful and need quick satisfaction of their urge. Infatuation is quick and easy, flighty and flimsy and leaves trashy memories worthy for the dustbin. It has painful stings for an unsuspecting victim. It comes coated with strange and deceptive emotions and leaves the victim reeling in its sting sooner than later.

If you figure out that you would not like your partner in the next 40 years looking old and fat, then watch out what you feel now for them is infatuation or lust. If you don't genuinely like your mate, sooner than later you are going to be miserable and perhaps regret the union. Lasting relationships are not built on infatuation or lust but on genuine and undeceiving love.

There is great contrast between love and lust. True love is neither physical nor romantic, it takes its time to grow;

while lust rushes and becomes full bloom quickly. Lust is either a sexual or very greedy feeling, while love is more of a secure and content filled feeling which we get by giving and receiving and caring for the one we love. Lust is more of an inordinate selfishness to possess and lacks depth of purpose. Lust can be a violent passion and ignores moral principles; after being satisfied, it has potentials to hurt others because it is a superficial feeling.

Love is kind, considerate, caring, giving, thoughtful, understanding, while lust is a temporary craving and greedy desire. Lust is often associated with certain addictions. When a relationship is based on lust, it may not stand the test of time.

You should be able to sort out through your emotions to honestly tell yourself whether it is love or lust that you are feeling for someone and this will guide you in your decision making. What feels like love may be mere physical attraction which is a very fragile foundation for a relationship or marriage. This is the reason people fall in love quickly and also fall out of love. Relationships that are likely to lead to marriage will have these ingredients - trust, respect, commitment, shared interests and reciprocated love.

Unreciprocated love is an issue of life which many people go through in the process of living and loving. It can, therefore, be safely said that it is a part of life. These experiences are meant to shape us and perhaps not destroy us. It may indeed make us more formidable and give us a bigger picture of what life is.

The fear that our love will be rejected or will not be reciprocated, sometimes stop us approaching the person we really like. In instances as these, "rejection is the curse and confidence is the cure". It is necessary to get into relationships that are sensible. The human being is a selfish animal and sometimes unduly possesses the object of love in a crazy fashion which can be as foolish as it is destructive. The truth is that some people are "madly in love" and stupid and they are most like to hurt the object of their love with the slighted provocation. Self-control and "sensible loving" should be exercised; so that people will be careful in how easily they give themselves.

Rationality and decent behavior should guide true love. On a first date, it is necessary not to get into sexual activity so that the romance is not short lived. Give time to knowing yourselves and finding out the extent the relation would go before indulging in sexual relations with your date. Let your date have something sizzling to look forward to on the next meeting. This also prolongs the excitement of the next meeting. When rationality is employed, people's emotions will be stable and under considerable control.

Chapter

12

Romantic Rejection

Oh
Where is my beloved?
I am held captive
By the one I love.
I called my beloved and he gave me no answers
Please don't go!!!

Romantic rejection is when someone knows you love him/her and simply does nothing and ignores you completely. It is unreciprocated love and it involves an individual rejecting someone in the context of a romantic relationship. It is a devastating feeling; where someone who has displayed love to the other person receives the "silent treatment." This indicates that the other person is not interested. Romantic rejection is like torture, very painful, very frustrating and makes the other person feel small, worthless and unwanted; hence issues of the heart have to be safely guarded; so that such traumatic feelings are avoided. Romantic rejection can cause depression and low self-esteem and it is a stab on someone emotions.

Unreciprocated love gives you a rebuff and this could have health implications on the person who is giving and seeking love. Rejection is an interpersonal situation where someone "throws back" insensitively without an acceptance or when someone refuses the romantic advances of another. It manifests in different forms like not showing up on a date, or moves out of the home, or ends an existing relationship or being unfaithful to one's partner. This could also manifest in rebuffing, ignoring and shunning the romantic advances of the other person. In other words, unreciprocated love is a "shut door" to the romantic advances of someone. It is an excruciating experience, hence, it is advisable to get encouraging responses before falling head over heels in love with someone; so that you do not waste that awesome feeling.

Unreciprocated love can lead to some adverse psychological consequences like loneliness, desperation, anger, despair, humiliation, fear of future rejection, reduced self-esteem, anxiety, depression, pain, aggression and insecurity. This is an emotionally painful experience because of the social nature of human beings and the basic need of being accepted and acknowledged. The need for love and belongingness is a fundamental human motivation. Giving and receiving love is psychologically healthy. Mere social interaction with people is not enough to fulfill this human need. Stable and caring interpersonal relationships are a basic human requirement for good health and happiness.

Life is, however, full of surprises and expectations. It also presents its fair share of disappointments. Persons you have entrusted with hopes, desires and feelings have turned around and said that they no longer want personal involvement with you. This could be devastating and it is as puzzling as it is bewildering. May be it is the way, your shape or height, your hair do and fashion, or the way you acted or the things you said or the things you did say that caused the rejection. Loving is sensitive and as such in expressing love, the emphasis should be on who wants us and not who we want. This is a priceless guide that will ameliorate incidences of romantic rejection.

Unreciprocated love is an issue of life which many people go through in the process of living and loving. It can, therefore, be safely said that it is a part of life. These experiences are perhaps meant to give us diverse perspectives of life and not to destroy us. It may indeed make us more formidable. People fall to rise up again in life. Fear of our love being rejected or not being reciprocated sometimes stops us from approaching the person we really like. This attitude will limit us and may build walls and barriers that will prevent people from reaching us.

Being good at your job/business, being organized and well dressed and in good shape are building blocks of self-confidence and it is a sort of coping mechanism in times when our love has not been reciprocated. However, when one has been rejected, the person has a tendency to come back stronger over time because it takes you into a time of reflection and thoughtfulness, envisioning new perspectives and inner learning. Learning is a lifelong phenomenon and we learn through diverse experiences.

This is not altogether an injurious phenomenon because it sometimes is a useful process which allows us to learn about ourselves. Although unreciprocated love hurts, be rest assured that you will get over it; because time heals all wounds and erases bad memories. It will bother you for a while; but life goes on and more often than not, you may meet someone that's meant just for you; that will bring sunshine into your life; that person that could be your soul mate.

When love is unreciprocated, it ignites different reactions from both sexes and sometimes issues of ego and past experiences contribute to certain extreme reactions. Most people like being loved and most also hate not being liked. Some people can't handle such situations; they simply go crazy. Men are more likely to react with aggression and want to hurt their female spouses or partners when they are faced with this type of situation.

In the United States alone, over a million women are "stalked" by their former boyfriends or husbands. Some people could do outrageous things, something of a rebound to exact some form of revenge. Women sometimes go into hiding or change residences or run into shelters for fear of aggression from their partners. Unfortunately some desperate partners stealthily pursue their "prey" to a conclusive and destructive end. Eight out of ten such women are physically attacked in these circumstances as an act of revenge. Some women get killed in these vengeful acts from their male counterparts and it is a gross waste of the female species. Women react less violently, most of the time, when faced with situations like this.

In relationships and affairs of the heart, caution should be exercised. In broadening this exposition, be prepared to face the little surprises that your friends and beloved ones spring at you once in a while. A good percentage of persons whose love is unreciprocated is because they have fallen in love with someone who has higher aspirations and is probably also on a higher social strata; hence care should be taken to try loving persons that belong to the same social stratification as you. If this happens, brace yourself, therefore, for any surprises that love and loving can present because there's no perfect person and the human being is a highly unpredictable and complex animal.

Tips On Handling Unreciprocated Love

1. Do not let it get to you or eat you up.

2. Forgive and forget and move on with great expectations.

3. You may cry to let out tears because crying is a human activity that brings relief paradoxically.

4. Try springing back to effectiveness. Keep busy at work, school or develop some leisure.

5. Try talking to someone on issues of common interest.

6. Make a check list of your weaknesses and deficiencies and turn them into a positive force. Try working on them; like upgrading your looks; changing your style of making your feelings known to the opposite sex, making better presentations etc.

7. Keep things in perspective by looking at the many positive aspects of your life.

8. Keep a good sense of humor, have an open mind and keep your confidence bubbling and the right person will be around sooner than you can imagine

Chapter

13

Teen Pregnancy

Teen pregnancy is an underage girl (under the age of 17) becoming pregnant. Teen pregnancy suggests unprotected sexual activity and it has high potentials for sexually transmitted diseases and the dreaded HIV/AIDS. Discovery of pregnancy for a teen is a scary and life changing event. When teens give birth, their future prospects and those of their children decline and usually teenage pregnancy carries a social stigma in many communities and cultures when it occurs outside marriage. Some families may go to the extreme by excommunicating the pregnant teen which may cause harm or exposure to harzards.

Teen pregnancy has become a social menace with a record of a teaming number of teens becoming "early mothers" due to frivolous and uncontrollable sexual urges and desires. Most teens become pregnant because they are naïve and do not understand their sexuality. Teen mothers are more likely to drop out from school or to die in pregnancy. Poverty and depression become more likely for them in those circumstances. Pregnant teens may have to set aside school and other personal priorities for their child because taking care of one's own child is a full time job. The fact is that teens are still growing up mentally and physically and as such, they do not know how to deal with issues of parenting.

For reasons of unpreparedness to attend fully to a new born, some girls/women opt for the drastic choice of baby dumping which is a most inhumane act since the baby invariably could die from dehydration, infections, lack of energy and calorie reserves. For these so individualized and complex reasons, girls/women kill these young members of our society who may be great personalities or accomplished professionals that the world will ever know. To this effect, governments should have centers where women should release such babies without prosecution implications; so that there will be more chances for babies exposed to the baby dumping phenomenon to live their God given lives.

Realistically, dealing with the responsibility of being a parent is one of the hardest tasks to take on as a young person. Becoming a teen parent automatically gives you a big responsibility to deal with and it involves emotions, dedication, patience and being able to financially support the child. Hence it is best to become a parent when you are old and mature enough to take on the responsibility. It is good to inform that many children especially off springs of unplanned pregnancies are in vulnerable conditions and rapidly deteriorate if emergent relevant interventions are delayed or unavailable. Issues of social menace and malaise are rampant causing great disruptions in society. Children from unplanned pregnancy are also more likely to become vagrant psychotics and delinquents.

Pregnant teenagers face many of the same obstetric issues that older women face and are more prone to risks during pregnancy than older women. Medical concerns for young mothers in the underdeveloped world are those of malnutrition and poor medical facilities. Conditions like the VVF become possible for these young mothers which could cause a life-long discomfort for the young mother, thereby, disrupting her chances for school and gainful employment and decent living. Teen pregnancy is one of the problems in today's society and it is fast becoming a global problem with the United States of America having the highest incidences of teen pregnancy in the developed world.

As a parent, finding out that your teen is pregnant can cause shock and despair and as a result, parents are advised to be pro-active. Helping your teens learn important lessons of the responsibility of teen parenting and the complications of teen pregnancy is a parental expectation. Parents should know that parental responsibility is to help prevent their female children from getting pregnant or their male children getting someone pregnant. This can be easily achieved by being approachable so that your teens can confidently have conversations; keeping the doors of communication sufficiently open; inculcate healthy family values; encourage fun activities and sports; know who your teenager is hanging out with; make your home an open place for your teenager's friends and talk

with them about the dangers of risky behavior and sexual diseases.

Parents should also take advantage of teachable moments when they watch television programs with their kids that have high content of adult concerns. Because adolescents spend a significant amount of time watching television, media and internet programs with high sexual content should be monitored and controlled. Adolescents who watch programs with a high level of exposure to video and television shows with high sexual content are more likely to get pregnant or impregnate someone.

Government departments of health and human services and non- profit organizations around the world are constantly advised to promote programs that help raise awareness of the gains of abstinence. There should be media censorship of programs that have high sexual content because it has undue influences on young minds and programs that show negative consequences, such as sexually transmitted diseases and unwanted pregnancies should be projected because it is highly educational for teens. Teenagers have a high sexual drive at this delicate period of their lives and educational programs that teach them about the implications of risky behaviors should be emphasized in schools and the society at large.

Chapter 14

Dashed Hopes

Carol And Jonathan

Carol was a year two undergraduate student when she met Jonathan. She gave her heart and undiluted love to Jonathan with promises to love him for the rest of her life. Jonathan was affluent and influential and bore the financial responsibility to see Carol through school. Carol's parents were poor and could not afford much for Carol's school fees and provisions. Carol under pressure to complete her education at the University, continued in the relationship for the sole reason of financial benefits. This cleared indicates in no uncertain terms that she was in the relationship for convenience rather than true love. She was not in love with Jonathan; however, she professed to love him. It was an extreme outward display of love and emotions and Jonathan was most unsuspecting. Jonathan would take her on shopping sprees overseas and to the best restaurants and wineries. Her school vacations were spent with Jonathan in his posh home which overlooked the Tennessee lakes. At evening, the twosome would relax in the coolness of the patio which overlooks the lake. It was high maintenance and sweet co-habitation with Jonathan. She shuttled to school for classes and tutorials from his exquisite residence. It was awesome comfort and she had everything she needed just for the asking. Jonathan was sincerely in love with Carol; but Carol was with him for the good things of life that would keep her going. She was highly deceptive and concealed her real self and acted love all the way.

Jonathan suddenly needed medical attention for severe pains and discomfort. Sooner than later, his health condition began to deteriorate and he was taken to the hospital for medical examination and treatment. He kept up a good demeanor since he was with the best doctors in town. A month later, Jonathan was diagnosed with hepatitis and HIV/AIDs. He was to stay in the hospital for a while for expert supervision and to be administered the full course of treatment.

Alas, Carol's world came crashing for the obvious reasons that she could be a carrier of the most dreaded HIV/AIDs virus due to her intimate relationship with Jonathan. They had unprotected sex so many times. As Jonathan was hospitalized in the Intensive Care Unit of the hospital, Carol was beginning to manifest symptoms of severe fever, pains and weakness of the body. A devastated Carol was also admitted into the hospital for the early stages of the disease. She also had complications of insomnia, a mental health condition. Jonathan never recovered and Carol hung onto faith for the best that the world can give to her perhaps for a few days, a few weeks or a few months as the case may be.

This scenario is what persons who love for the wrong reasons go through sometimes. They find themselves "pushed to the wall" by life's circumstances and fake love for reasons of convenience and survival. They are not aware of the health information of their partner and they go all out to "dig the gold mine". They throw caution to the wind and maintain sometimes life-long relationships that are devoid of loving emotions that can stand the test of time. They act out emotions to confuse and to deceive their partners; they have no experience of what sweet and loving interactions are. They stay through life "holed" up in a love-less relationship for shady reasons, most of the time unnoticed by their unsuspecting partners. They share the marital vows with sinister intentions and mortify their flesh and feelings for vain and well thought out reasons. They scheme through the union for as long as they can, living with it in silent pain as mercenaries. Sometimes, they do not count the cost of a life-long agony. They persevere in the conflicting feelings until death do them part as their marriage vows connote.

The other side of the coin is that there is so much to gain for true love. True love is sharing the depths of your heart's warmth with someone. True love is a candid feeling and tender affection towards someone. It is soothing, enduring, and pleasurable with implications for healthy romantic living and a good long life. It is worth searching for and waiting for until it comes; so that intimacy will be most refreshing and life worth living. Intimacy is a close, familiar and affectionate relationship with your spouse. It is an elating feeling that gives joyful sustenance and longevity to life and relationships. True love is comforting and priceless.

Chapter

15

Choosing A Partner

Selecting a life-long partner is the most important decision an adult can make in life. Thoughtful considerations and knowing what you want in your life and in a relationship can prepare you for choosing a lasting one. A lasting marriage portends one that has minimal conflicts, physical, psychological and mental health problems. A traumatic marriage could be worse than the pangs of loneliness that singles face. A traumatic marriage could have health implications and could mean a world of shattered dreams.

The world reels in pain as reports of spousal murder, brutalities, divorce, domestic violence, legal battles over property, alimony and custody of children are blared daily over the mass media. Female partners on flight seeking for refuge at obscure shelters and dormitories to avoid assault or death from their enraged partners along with law suits and domestic wrangles become the unfortunate decimals of one time loving relationships.

Choosing a life time partner, therefore, is a milestone event and it calls for caution and self-control from raging and uncontrollable emotions. An honest assessment and dispassionate judgment of your intended partner should take the place of hasty and lustful decisions. In choosing a partner, issues of age should, as a matter of fact, not stand as bottlenecks since it is becoming culturally acceptable for considerable age differential to exist between couples. This is becoming even more fashionable and a common occurrence in human societies today.

Before making a choice of a life time partner, it is important that intending couples have effective communication and hold honest conversations about career, money, dreams, goals, expectations, vacations, religion etc. Marriage is a serious life time commitment, therefore, the period prior to marriage is a period of assessing your partner's temperament and ability to hold conversations on issues that resonate often in marriage.

If your partner evades conversations, you must re-think your decisions in order to avoid future marital conflicts. Emotions and uncontrollable desire have potentials to becloud judgment in the process of making choices, therefore, they should be under control as much as possible so that carefully considered and rational decisions can be made. When someone is caught in the web of loving, sweet feelings of the partner most often than not control the emotions. People are not able to "see clearly until the rain the gone". Sometimes, the oversight takes a chunk of the person's happiness for the rest of life and it becomes most regrettable.

Courtship is a social process that precedes marriage which socializes both sexes into accepting possible forms of a fruitful relationship. Sometimes families organize and supervise courtships; while in more recent years most courtships are arranged outside the family circle. The world is moving at a very fast paced rate and this affects every area of people's lives. People meet in clubs, social gatherings, beaches, shopping centers and malls and as fast as the micro oven, make commitments to marry. Some of the time, the relationship is taken into quick sex and the stage is set for a quick marriage without the consent of family members.

Women by nature are known to trigger courtship through non-verbal behaviors (body language) which men could respond to as the case may be.

In choosing a partner, girls and women generally should understand that there is something known as "male behavior". This is experienced by all women; but when it comes to women with very high IQs, males sometimes display a form of meanness known as male behavior. Typically, men want lower status women. They avoid women of higher status because they will often feel that makes the woman more desirable than they are themselves. Women of high status tend to be more vocal and independent as well. That is when a man is likely to be aggressive as a means of asserting control over the woman. In the United States alone, three women are killed daily by their spouses or male partners. This is very pitiful and calls for extra caution in making partner choices.

Psychologists have confirmed that when a man unleashes aggressive behavior on a woman like demeaning her, it will make the woman feel low, neglected and disrespected. Consequent, if the woman feels humiliated, she will eventually come to believe that she cannot do any better and she will tend to stick around with that man. It is a classic cycle of subtle abuse; and surprisingly this appears to be happening to a lot of brilliant women.

Highly educated women (clever women) are sometimes naïve when it comes to emotional matters and they are too easily fooled by men; because they have spent their time mainly in libraries while their less clever counterparts are busy learning and mastering the art of knowing how to figure men out.

Not surprising we have some women who dominate boardrooms; women who have distinguishing business awards who are still very much single, in deep romantic misery because they have not mastered the art of sensible choice making like they mastered intellectual pursuits.

Some of these career women who can't pick the right guy tend to be embarrassed that they keep getting it wrong romantically.

Helpful Tips

It is good to have some information about the health of your prospective partner. Ascertaining the blood group and HIV status of your partner is a good one. Knowing the cholesterol level of your partner could actually help you in honestly planning his/her diet. Remember that getting married is not just for sex and romance. It is also caring for the health and other interests of your partner. With useful information at your fingertips, your decision now become informed and carefully thought out and surprises and suspicions are minimized in marriage.

People oftentimes react to "chemistry" to make choices of a life partner. While "chemistry" is an essential ingredient, this all important decision requires more than just chemistry. "Opposites attract" may be true; infatuation may be true too, but these do not usually lead to lengthy partnerships. They are transient feelings that may burn out quicker than expected.

It requires thoughtful considerations and assessing your partner if both of you are resonating on the same social strata. Most happy long lasting partnerships are formed by people who are similar. A similar social-economic, religious, ethnic and racial background of couples is beneficial but does not guarantee the survival of a marriage. However, people who share common backgrounds, values, interests, hobbies and similar social networks are better suited as marriage partners than people who are very different in their backgrounds and networks.

Hence, your delights and past times should be things that interest your prospective partner; so that there will be reduced areas of conflict. When the thoughts and ideas of couples harmonize, they become a happier couple and may have a healthier relationship. Couples with major differences are most likely candidates of separation and divorce at some point in their married life.

Tips For Choosing A Partner

An essential tip in choosing a partner is to make your standards "human" rather than "material." You have to look out for the things that are tangible and not the mundane things; so that you are not plunged into a life of unfulfilled dreams and romantic misery. Men are more visual and physical; and they tend to look out for physical features in a woman first rather than the substance. In this regard, men ought to be very careful and exercise self-control; so that their assessments of their-would-be partners are not beclouded by sentiments. It is good to be dispassionate at some point before matrimony in order to thoughtfully consider one's decisions of choice; because that singular decision could make or mar the entire life process.

For a relationship to pass the test there should be more than just physical attraction. It is essential to understand as much a possible that there is a huge difference between being "in love" and being in a good love relationship:

1. In choosing a partner, ascertain the HIV status of your partner.

2. In choosing a partner, know that as a teenager, you are at a high risk of failure in your intended relationship or marriage because of poor judgment.

3. A stable mind and one with an ability to hold a steady job.

4. Avoid getting into "trial marriage" or cohabiting before you think you can make a choice; because the mystery of yourself is cheaply unveiled and there is no excitement to look forward to by each of you.

5. Don't just accept who so ever is willing to be with you. Look out for the best. It is not how early to make the choice of your life partner, it is usually how best suited to you the choice is.

6. Don't let your choice be money and material driven. There are many millionaires that make very unpleasant partners.

7. Don't choose on the basis of pity.

8. Don't choose because you are being pressured by external forces to do so; because this is a choice for a life time.

9. Can you cope with his/her temperament?

10. Never choose a partner that consistently undermines you or makes your unhappy.

11. Observe how he/she treated last partner, family, friends and those close to him. Know that people do not spontaneously make major changes in how they behave. Generally people do not change a great deal. See people for who they are and not what you want them to be.

12. Choose a partner that will satisfy your long term needs. What you need "right now" are your short term needs and what you will always need in life are your long term needs.

13. Be honest to differentiate between infatuation and love. Observe the level of reciprocity of his/her love.

14. Know what you need and ascertain if a potential partner can meet with your needs.

15. Be clear of what you mean by an ideal relationship and figure out if your potential partner can give you anything near that.

16. Do not live in a world of fantasy. Unrealistic expectations could ruin your decision making; so be sensible and realistic in your expectations and in setting your parameters.

17. Marry your best friend, somebody that understands your innate being and somebody that likes you for who you are; somebody you can trust and who will be willing to go the extra mile for your sake.

Chapter

16

Partner Choices And Consequences

When choices are made in this all important milestone of choosing lifetime partners, there are inevitable consequences. When good choices have been made in this regard, life becomes meaningful, kids are raised in stable home settings with its attendant benefits, couples have better health and have a better environment to attain career objectives and other life goals and aspirations. When good choices have been made, there is visible radiance exuding from the couple and this is most ideal.

Happiness, friendship and romance bubble in the union and dreams including career goals are more often times realized under benign conditions. Healthy interaction forms the bedrock of a lasting union and couples are likely to get into jubilee celebrations of their marriage thereby being true to their marital vows to love and cherish each other for as long as they live.

Now this is my philosophy, you have to work hard with your feelings, your emotions and your heart in order to feel or get to experience the real, pure, intense love and affection for someone that you know you want to be with and this does not happen in a day. It takes effort to make a marriage or relationship work and last for a long time.

However, when poor choices have been made, situations become different, difficult and disastrous. Life becomes a tale of woes for the couple and ugly consequences become inevitable. The sad reality is that these consequences could go on for a life time which could be injurious and life threatening with undertones of guilt and regret.

Unfortunately, at this time, one cannot put back the hands of the clock!

At the point of decision making, extreme caution should be exercised because the decisions you make will define your future. Unfortunately, some people are signing their "death warrants" by the choices they make. Short of being killed in marriage, is also a possibility of physical or psychological brutalities which could result in physical health conditions or mental health break downs. It cannot be overemphasized that you have to say "Yes, I do" with someone you really like, someone that will suit you, someone you feel comfortable with; someone that accepts you for who you are and not just someone to make love to or someone who is rich or someone who just looks good.

Hence, there are grave consequences if the parameters for choices are based on physical attraction and material possessions instead of on being compatible and able to resonate on the same social strata with your intended life partner. Choices define whether one will be married for a life time with one spouse, or get into serial monogamy or live as a single person or single parent etc.

The need for caution cannot be over emphasized because every-one wants a good life and a good marriage. Some people cannot cope with conflicts for a long period of time. Tolerance levels are different and people react in diverse ways in times of conflict. On signing the dotted lines saying "Yes, I do" with a life partner, it may be placing a death sentence on oneself. This has kept the police and homicide detectives busy in the world today as they respond minute to minute to calls for help from one time lovers. In some cases, children and other family members are involved in the turbulence and this entirely contradicts the very essence of marriage. Evidence of increased divorce rates are also clearly seen through empirical observations in friends and family circles which leaves much to be desired.

It is true that more of the time, children suffer a whole lot more than their parents in these unsavory situations caused by divorce and separation. They could become dysfunctional kids or get into depression, poor school performances, bad peer groupings, drugs and alcohol, vagrant or other questionable behaviors. It is a serious situation for one time lovers being engaged in deadly fights. When love turns to hate, couples could go to any length to vent their anger or vengeance on themselves.

Research has it that every minute one woman is killed by a spouse or boyfriend somewhere in the world. This is regrettable and heartbreaking because it depletes the female specie on a minute to minute basis. This gory situation is also the reason some people choose celibacy or prefer to remain single or become single parents. Although issues of loneliness may crop up, tranquility will be the outcome of being marriage averse and they live determined to be happy and maintain their sanity.

Fundamentally, most of these situations arise due to low frustration tolerance. Patience levels appear very low between couples in the present time and age. Issues that otherwise would have been resolved amicably with enduring conversation degenerate into deadly violence leading to physical or psychological injury, maiming or death of one of the partners who once had shared marital vows publicly when solemnizing their unions or had life time commitments to themselves when they agreed to share their lives.

In the United States alone, the daily statistics are that one male is killed by a wife or girlfriend while three women are killed by their current or past spouses or boyfriends as the case may be. Deadly weapons have also been reported to have been used. As unfortunate as this is, it is a sad reality that men who should protect women with their God given superior energy use it to destroy women every minute according to research findings.

As people begin to live together, a kind of unwritten political struggle gradually unfolds. Subtle issues of decision making in every area of matrimonial life are tackled diplomatically or otherwise and there is a silent "muscle flexing" as the case may be. Hence, careful considerations should be made before choices are made. Sometimes, the violence takes place within the home and sometimes, one partner stalks the other unknowingly to unleash injury or death. This leaves much to be desired of a hitherto loving relationship where partners had pledged to love, cherish and be together for the rest of their lives.

There could be emotional drama of heartbreak when the supposed life partner is not leaving to expectations. All these could have been figured out during dating and courtship, hence, it is fundamental to be honest to one self when such epoch decisions are being made. In order to avoid these traumatic sequences, try figuring out if your partner has violent tendencies, if you are really compatible with your partner and observe the possible things your partner could do under provocation or in conditions of extreme stress and provocation.

Scholars researching in this paradoxical situation where lovers or couples brutalize their partners rest it on the fact that they have many differences than similarities. When couples do not have the same things that excite them and their interests are far apart, conflict may be the order of the day in their day to day relationship. This gradually takes its toll on the feelings of the couple for each other and they may no longer feel the same as they did towards themselves in the beginning. Their relationship begins to come under undue pressure and there may be romantic rejections.

Sometimes, couples have not had honest conversations before giving their consent for marriage. They have either been carried away by infatuation or lust for each other and did not make good decisions. Their unbridled emotions at that time beclouded their sense of good judgment and they have to face the ugly consequences of their decisions. Most times couples have not taken time to understand the temperament of their partners and to be able to figure out how the other person can react when provoked or under pressure or deprivation.

It, therefore, becomes a case of sensible loving when persons with similar social circumstances, educational and financial attainments tie the nuptial knots. In broadening this conversation, it is crucial for couples to be able to talk together at all times, have similar or same interests, past times, hobbies and similar life goals and dreams. This will reduce areas of conflict as much as possible. In fact it is advisable to marry your best friend, someone you can have a good laugh with, someone you can talk to without inhibitions, someone who understands who you are and the things you like.

Marrying for reasons other than true love may be dangerous and disastrous in the long run. This is because true love portends a more enduring union and justifies the marriage vows. True love no doubt is a solid foundation to build a life time with someone. True love is a combination of the passionate love and the compassionate love. True love is not just ecstasy and sex; it is truly caring and being able to take care of the other person's interest. True love when nourished by couples, can stand the test of a life time.

Divorces and separation are caused when couples realize no sooner than later that they are incompatible in many areas and indeed have no business being together.

This presents a somewhat dicey situation and becomes the foundation of marital conflicts, separation, divorce, domestic violence, emotional or health problems as the case may be.

One major consequence of making an erroneous choice is that happiness becomes elusive. This becomes the devil's "workshop" because it could lead to a state of being mentally divorced with your partner and consequent infidelity and relationship break up. The human being has a tendency of looking for solutions to problems in the wrong places thinking that "the grass is greener on the other side." Most of the time, the grass is not really greener with the other person and it triggers a cycle of serial monogamy with people getting into their second, third, fourth, and fifth marriages.

Where children are involved and things have fallen apart, it brings along with it unimaginable pressure on kids and the thorny phenomenon of single parenthood.

Some persons do not have natural capacity to cope with marital stress for a long time; so they readily and willingly throw in the towel and seek comfort in other places. Hasty and faulty decisions are bound to be made in a bid to seek emotional satisfaction somewhere else hence sound and dispassionate considerations should be made at the time of making choices for life partners because it is one of the most important decisions in life.

Poor choices of life time partners could also have health implications. This is because incessant conflicts eventually could lead to frustration, sleep problems, confusion, trauma, anxiety attacks, heart problems, high blood pressure, mental health break downs, physical health problems and possible suicide or spousal homicide as the case may be.

Chapter

17

Irony Of Wedding Vows

Wedding Vows In Perspective

A wedding vow is a solemn and earnest declaration of love. It is a promise, a pledge and personal commitment to one's partner. It is an assertive statement of your feelings for your partner.

On this special day, I affirm to you in the presence of God and all those in attendance my sacred promise to stay by your side in sickness and in health, in joy and in sorrow, as well as through the good times and the bad times.

I (Bride/Groom) take you (Groom/Bride) to be my (wife/husband), to have and to hold from this day forward, for better or for worse, for richer, for poorer, in sickness and in health, to love and to cherish; from this day forward until death do us part.

I promise to love you without reservation, comfort you in times of distress, encourage you to achieve all of your goals, laugh with you and cry with you, grow with you in mind and spirit, always be open and honest with you and cherish you for as long as we both shall live.

I promise to love you without reservation, honor and respect you, provide for your needs as best I can, look out for your interests, protect you from harm, and comfort you in times of distress. So help me Lord.

Sometimes, the couples say in unison the following words:

Entreat me not to leave you, or to return from following after you, for where you go I will go, and where you stay I will stay. Your people will be my people and your God will be my God. And where you die, I will die and there I will be buried. May the Lord do with me and more if anything but death parts you from me.

Your wedding vows set the tone for your marriage. The heart and soul of your wedding are your vows to each other. Wedding vows are affirmations about love, life and partnership. Wedding vows indeed are romantic, unique and meaningful. The vows create a great wedding day experience. Ideally, the vows should flow from your heart and you should live your wedding vows and be that which you have promised your partner you will be him/her.

Wedding vows are supposed to affirm how great you feel having found the one perfect person for you, the one who suits you so comfortably and who gives you joy and hope and anticipation for the future. It is declaring your love and devotion to your spouse before members of family and friends and to the world at large. Wedding vows assure your spouse of the best of you from now until the very end. It establishes that you are one with your spouse; that your spouse is indeed beautiful to you, not just in face but in spirit also. Wedding vows mean extensively that your spouse is a seal over your heart.

Irony in this context means that the attitudes of some couples are the opposite of their wedding vows. Their character becomes incongruous with their vows in the course of the marriage. Their lifestyles and actions become totally inconsistent with their professed principles because their lives and the momentum of the marriage become the outcome of events contrary to what was expected.

Fundamentally, the human being is a complex animal, highly unpredictable and responds also to environmental stimuli. The quality of interaction and the level of understanding of couples have a lot to do in the success of their union and could in fact decide the percentage of harmony. In many marriages, the lives of the couples become visibly contrary to what was expected. This becomes ridiculous because friends and family that were present on the historic wedding day see a highly incongruous and distasteful scenario which leaves one in doubt of the sincerity of the vows that were shared on that eventful and historic day.

The case of Cindy and Harold is a reference point. They had a great wedding day that was witnessed by friends and family at the gardens of Meridian Hotels and Towers. The venue was decked with the most gorgeous décors of a great and romantic day for a twosome known for their sweet vows and intimate kisses on their day. There was a glitz and glamor and a rendition of the best soul and R & B music which delighted the wedding guests. It was celebrated with Champaign and a buffet of choice meals that guests attested was gracious.

Cindy had dated Harold for two years and they had great and frantic excitements towards each other. They demonstrated a public show of love and affection wherever they went. They had extravagant shopping sprees because Harold was affluent with a lot of inherited property from his father. His father was a rich merchant who had a shipping business. Their wedding day was a celebration that featured a galaxy of opera stars and varied entertainment for guests.

The couple settled into flamboyant living and enjoyed their vacations at great sites that are well known for their tourist attraction. They demonstrated their love and assured themselves of their commitment to a sweet union for the rest of their lives. Cindy had exquisite moments with Harold who appreciated her beauty and charm. Cindy is a blonde with bold blue eyes and high cheek bones. She also had an elegant poise and physique that is bewitching. She was sweetly romantic to her hussy and hero; but by the third anniversary of their wedding, Cindy was diagnosed with a heart condition that would see her in and out of hospital for a long time. This traumatized her a great deal and she became a fragile piece of beauty. She was no longer available to satisfy the desires of Harold for a spritely and elegant wife.

Harold got Cindy a health insurance to pay for her medical bills and eventually sued for divorce. Puzzled at the unsavory developments, Cindy reflected on her romance with Harold, her fabulous wedding day and their wedding vows "till death do us part". In her sorrowful state, she had a siege of pneumonia that debilitated her completely. She was, however, too ill to contest the divorce and Harold went ahead to marry Michelle, an accomplished model.

Chapter

18

Multiple Sex Partners

Many people change partners at least once, during their adult lives. Studies reveal that girls/boys now start having sex at younger ages and an earlier start to sexual intercourse often leads to multiple sexual partner behavior. At this stage, they are experimenting with their sexuality and intimacy. School drop outs are more culprits of risky sexual behaviors and they have no qualms in getting into multiple partnerships.

At any given time, a significant percentage of men are engaging in multiple sexual partnerships with women – a situation that facilitates the spread of sexually transmitted diseases. Even persons who are securely situated in relationships feel occasionally attracted to the outsider, regardless of the health implication sooner than later. This impulse to pursue sexual variety is timeless; could be trendy but very toxic to say the least. There are also situations where multiple partnerships run concurrently and this has huge implications; because it implies being in more than one sexual relationship at a time; and that perhaps multiple sexual relationships/activities are going on at the same time.

Noticeable trends at the moment see a high rate of concurrent sexual relationships and the fact that it poses great danger to humanity cannot be overemphasized. Concurrent sexual relationships are more common among unmarried men because of inordinate desire for sexual variety and experiences. Incessant multiple partnerships and concurrent sexual relationships can expose men to penal or erectile tissue damage. This behavior put these men and their partners at a higher risk of contracting the dreaded HIV/AIDs virus and other sexually transmitted diseases.

Multiple partnerships expose people to STD's, genital herpes and HIV/AIDs. This further implies having unprotected sex. At particular risk among people are sex workers; because their lifestyles often include high rates of partner change. This leads to an efficient spread of HIV and STD's, which progresses through broad sexual networks at very rapid rates, reaching multiple clients, children, spouses and associated sexual partners and other sex workers. Prostitution is as old as humanity and it poses grave danger to the entire society. It is using one's body indecently for a fee and prostitutes are unduly exposed to health and other life threatening hazards. It is a regrettable social menace.

Scientists believe that individuals that have oral sex with multiple partners are more likely to have cancer than those who do not indulge in oral sex. This is because through oral sex, partners may transmit certain viruses that cause cancer. Scientists have also established that there is a strong association between alcohol and drug use with the urge to have multiple partnerships. These substances cause exaggerated boldness, heightened libido and insatiable sexual appetites. People should consume them with utmost caution because additionally, they could lead to other physical and mental health conditions.

Singles participate more in sex work and sex workers are a most reluctant demographic in seeking out information or services for the prevention or care of infectious diseases; thereby making it difficult for society, governments, hospitals to reach them to curtail the spread of diseases through sexual networks.

The sex worker industry is an age old industry and it is becoming highly competitive because of younger entrants. In most human societies, sex workers are stigmatized and marginalized and treated as "second rate citizens" and so they prefer to be "invisible". Unfortunately, the health and social consequences of their life styles gets transmitted into the society and the world at large.

In choosing the next partner, there is usually scanty research and preparation. In fact people who want to buy a new car or technological gadget do more research to ensure the best buy than do people who are getting a new partner or getting into multiple partnerships.

Teenagers, who have sex with more than one partner in a short period of time, are likely to engage in other risky behaviors such as fighting, alcoholism, smoking, drugs etc. Having sexual intercourse with multiple partners increase the risk of pregnancy, sexually transmitted diseases and resulting damage to reproductive health. Women are more likely than men to become infected and tend to have more severe and longer-lasting symptoms. Women are also more prone to consequent complications. Multiple sexual partners increase the risk of women to have cervical cancer.

Yvonne dropped out of school because she was pregnant at 18. She eventually had a bouncing baby boy but preferred to put him up for adoption because she was not psychologically ready to be a parent. She lacked parenting skills and was financially incapacitated to provide adequately for the baby. She gave him up safely to the hospital authorities. She did not consider the option of baby dumping and its attendant hazards because she was morally obliged to give her baby the fundamental human right to life.

She later recuperated at a nursing home where she went to for post natal care. Her parents worked at the coal mines assiduously for the family upkeep. She had very little supervision and unhealthy peer interactions which further complicated her upbringing. She became a stripper at a club to make money for her upkeep and subsequently moved out of home into a brothel to fend for herself and to continue in her frivolous passion of prostituting, stripping and night club dancing. She used alcohol and sex enhancing drugs to support her life style of having multiple sex partners and night clubbing. It was fun as she would gyrate all night at the clubs dancing and stripping before a hilarious audience.

Yvonne lost contact with her parents who had reported to the police that she was missing.

Pictures of "missing Yvonne" were shown on both the electronic and print media. Her case brought a great puzzle to her parent, the police and entire community. The search for Yvonne continued and her parents wondered if she was to be counted among the dead.

Yvonne developed pain and feverish conditions following her life of drug overdose and frivolous sex. She traumatized with pain and began to emaciate rapidly. She scheduled to visit the hospital for thorough medical checkups. The physician confirmed that she was in the early stages of the dreaded HIV/AIDs disease. Huge doses of antibiotics were administered as well as life sustaining drugs to elongate her life and ameliorate the painful spasms which she suffered. Life became a harrowing experience and she would occasionally peep through the windows of her brothel to catch a glimpse of a beautiful world. She held unto life as she made weekly visits to the hospital to have her physicals done.

Her chosen profession demanded agility and vibrancy for effective stage performances. She was gradually loosing vigor and she could no longer withstand the rigors of stripping, dancing and sex work. She was going through financial difficulties; sickness and starvation stared her in the face; her friends and clients have dissipated into thin air. She was all alone in despair and with uncertain health conditions which deprived her of the "fun" of her chosen profession.

Dejected, beaten and battered by a debilitating disease, a gleam of hope flashed through her as she thought of finding her parents. Nostalgic feelings overwhelmed her and she remembered how she ate cucumbers in her little family home in upstate New York. She dispatched letters to her parents using express postal services explaining her dilemma and predicament and a bewildered mum came knocking on her doors at the brothel on a cold winter evening.

Chapter 19

Divorce

Divorce and dissolution of marriage is a legal process that leads to the end of a marriage. It is a judicial declaration dissolving a marriage and it releases the husband and wife from all matrimonial obligations. Divorce is a social phenomenon that should attract concerted attention due to the fact that divorced persons have become a growing demographic within the United States, Canada and Scandinavia having the highest divorce rates globally. Places like Italy and countries in Africa retain a lower divorce rates. Divorce is a social and environmental toxin and should be condemned in no uncertain terms.

A frightening percentage of first marriages end in divorce and second and third marriages are also hitting very high percentages. A known risk factor for divorce is marrying as a teenager and the world is witnessing a lot of teenage marriages as at this time. Studies reveal that divorce risk triples if one is from a family broken by divorce; suggesting ripple effects of divorce of off-springs. Risk of divorce is lower for people who wait to marry at least until their mid-twenties, people who have not lived together with different partners prior to marriage or people who are strongly religious and marry someone of the same faith.

Many may be getting married for the wrong reasons. Not knowing your partner well enough before marriage and having a low tolerance level and not giving enough time to reconcile differences are some of the reasons for a high rate of relationship break-ups. People who have multiple **cohabiting relationships** before marriage are more likely to experience conflict and eventual divorce than people who do not cohabit. Similar social-economic, religious, ethnic and racial backgrounds of couples are beneficial but it does not eliminate incidences of divorce. A high level commitment by a couple to make their marriage work is a crucial factor to survival of a marriage. Nurturing a union with sincerity and care from each of the partners is a spring that will make marriages evergreen.

There are laws to confirm the dissolution of this previous love bond where persons involved had shared a part of their lives and livelihood together. Divorce laws vary around the world, though divorce is not permitted in some countries and some religions, but annulment of marriage is permitted. In most jurisdictions, a divorce must be certified by a court of law to become effective.

Divorce is a thorny issue that has intense implications for families and society at large. This is because it involves emotions, feelings of betrayal, guilt, broken dreams, spousal support, child custody, child support, distribution of property, prenuptial and postnuptial agreements etc. As a most thorny and regrettable issue, divorce disrupts family life including too the lives of the children involved. The ripple effects of divorce are monumental and it is a very distasteful experience for couples who had shared so much together to be at war with each other. Candidly efforts should be made by couples to have a higher bar of frustration tolerance and patience.

Payment of legal fees, court appearances, fights for property and children custody disputes make divorce stressful in itself. Other methods of timely conflict resolution are also encouraged because of the long standing goals of healthy family relations and a better and more stabilized society. Some couples divorce hastily because they think that the grass will be greener on the other side. They look forward to new relationships that may portend a greater evil. Making a marriage work is in the interest of couples because divorce proceedings are clumsy, stressful and financially wasteful. Post-divorce could be even more stressful and volatile; hence high tolerance levels and self-control is suggested among couples and family interferences in the lives of couples should be minimized. Most of the time, there is no "friendly divorce" it is always surrounded by "tales of woe" and sometimes there are incidences of violence for couples with poor impulse control.

A divorce involves more than just a husband and wife. If there are children, they are involved as well as other family members. Most of the time, children are more prone to suffer adversely the consequences of divorce. Children bear the brunt of the "mess" and they could suffer psychological damage as a consequence. Children could develop maladjusted behavior and suffer from insecurity, depression, anger for the rest of their lives. This is the reason the judiciary has a pressing interest in divorce cases involving children; so that the disputes between parents do not spill over on them. The human angle recognized by most jurisdictions is to encourage a workable parenting plan. Children, however, could grow up confused about issues of life and loving when they get into joint custody situations of being with each parent at different times.

Some couples contest divorce while others do not bother to go through the messy court proceedings. Contested divorce may be stressful to spouses and lead to expensive litigations. There are adversarial and less adversarial approaches to divorce issues. Less adversarial approaches have emerged in recent times such as mediated and collaborative divorce where there are mutually acceptable resolutions to issues of conflict. In the event of divorce being grossly inevitable on grounds of irreconcilable differences, trying to work together to end a marriage will be the easiest and most thoughtful way to save money.

Divorce, custody and support cases can be very expensive for the parties involved. Hiring Lawyers to "fight it out" may be a waste of funds that could have been invested for long and short term dividends. Getting a divorce is emotional enough and even more devastating when gross legal expenses are involved. In some cases, legal proceedings to effect a divorce are easy and timely in order to avoid issues of domestic violence. In this case non judiciary administrative entities are suggested to certify a divorce in cases where divorce is mutually acceptable to the parties involved.

Consequences Of Divorce

Divorce is not easy for the people involved. For majority of the time, divorce is extremely painful, disorganizing and could have health and security implications. It causes ugly flashbacks and painful memories. Its disadvantages far outweigh the advantages if any. It is best avoided. The grass is not always greener on the other side. Consequences of a divorce:

1. Regret, depression, anger, frustration, anguish, bitterness, hatred, insecurity etc.

2. It can have long term effects on new relationships.

3. It can destroy self-esteem.

4. Fear about the future.

5. Breakdown of family relationship.

6. Stress on off-springs of marriage.

Coping Tips:

1. Seek faith based counsel and help from your religious institution and get involved in more faith based activities. This facilitates the healing process because healing of the mind and body is required most of the time for both parties.

2. Deal with your ex-wife or ex-husband in a civil way whenever occasion presents.

3. Try as much as possible to keep company of friends and family members; in order to avoid pitiful and suicidal thoughts.

4. Develop a vision, a passion for example care giving to the needy, care for the sick, widows and elderly etc. This helps you assess the problems of others and this could bring comfort to your aching heart.

5. Treat yourself often to long walks, visit the parks, movies, eating out, window shopping, sing and listen to music of choice as much as possible, read delightful literature and materials and fill up the void in your mind.

6. Feel good about you and pamper yourself for brief moments

7. Reach out to others and talk to people that can relate and empathize and avoid people that would put you down.

8. Don't be hasty to get into new emotional relationships. Some people have waded through second, third and fourth divorces. Divorce from one partner does not guarantee the success of the next relationship. Endeavor to have more information and know more about prospective partners so as to help you make informed and wise decisions.

9. Remove your wedding pictures from your view. It will help you to go through the rebuilding

process faster. Living and loving continues for the hopeful.

10. Be positive of a bright future. If sleep problems set in, consult a physician. These are human reactions to shattered hopes and dreams of your wedding day. A day you made your wedding vows to love and to cherish your partner for the rest of your lives. Feel good.

Divorce is most unsavory. Consequently, society and the media should adopt programs that promote healthy marriages for purpose of bequeathing a healthy legacy to upcoming generations. Religious institutions, the larger society should enrich existing marriages and efforts should be made to restore troubled marriages as well in the communities. Having "Mentor couples" is, hereby, propagated for purposes of assuring couples that long lasting marriages are possible. This has potentials to reduce the rates of separation and divorce to the barest minimum in congregations and communities.

The Marriage Tonic

1. Try smiling more in your marriage. Smiling represents a positive disposition towards life and has the potentials to lighten a heavy mood.

2. Be empathetic. Listen to your partner and give empathetic responses to the content of the message you are receiving.

3. Think about what you are hearing before you respond.

4. Respond nicely using perhaps these words "I really appreciate your concern and the way you feel". Positive response could encourage your partner.

5. Resolve conflicts quickly.

6. Spend quality time with each other, enjoy your past times and hobbies together.

7. Complement yourselves.

8. Re-live your pre-marriage romances; date yourselves once in a while by going on vacations, eating out occasionally and visiting fun places together.

9. Visualize your partner romantically and add play to your everyday lives.

10. Dress to make your spouse happy.

11. Do not take yourselves for granted.

12. Celebrate yourselves.